YES
VE-GAN!

GAIA
MANIFESTO

YES VE-GAN!

A BLUEPRINT FOR VEGAN LIVING

Selene Nelson

To my mother,
for planting that first seed

An Hachette UK Company
www.hachette.co.uk

First published in Great Britain in 2019 by Gaia,
an imprint of Octopus Publishing Group Ltd
Carmelite House
50 Victoria Embankment
London EC4Y 0DZ
www.octopusbooks.co.uk

Distributed in the US by
Hachette Book Group
1290 Avenue of the Americas
4th and 5th Floors
New York, NY 10104

Distributed in Canada by
Canadian Manda Group
664 Annette Street
Toronto, Ontario, Canada M6S 2C8

ISBN 978-1-85675-427-9

A CIP catalogue record for this book is available from
the British Library.

Printed and bound in the United Kingdom.

1 3 5 7 9 10 8 6 4 2

Publishing Director: Stephanie Jackson
Art Director: Juliette Norsworthy
Senior Editor: Sarah Reece
Copyeditor: Jo Smith
Globe illustration: Claire Huntley
Production Controller: Emily Noto

MIX
Paper from
responsible sources
FSC® C018072

Contents

MY VEGAN JOURNEY

20 August 2017. That was the date I went vegan, the date a new chapter of my life started. It was the date I made the most transformative and profound decision of my life – though of course, I didn't know it then. I was already vegetarian by this point, so I didn't imagine going vegan would be a life-changing decision. I just thought I wasn't going to be eating cheese and eggs any more.

I was – quite randomly – in Abu Dhabi at the time, on a five-day stopover at the end of a long period of travelling. After months of thinking about 'maybe kind of going part-time vegan', something in my mind just clicked. I was ready. But it had been a long time coming.

Looking back on my 'vegan journey' now, I can see that it didn't start in August 2017 in Abu Dhabi. It actually started a few years before, in November 2014, in Williamsburg, NYC. I was visiting family when I came across a stray cat in the street – a rare sight in New York. As I stroked it and wondered whose it was, a woman rushed out. She was worried about the cat, and we started talking. This woman was a vegan and an animal activist, and she told me she'd just returned from an anti-fur protest outside a celebrity book signing.

'I'm vegetarian!' I said, wanting her to know that I, too, loved animals. 'And I try to only buy high-quality cheese and eggs, from ethical farms.' (Oh, how that sentence would come back to haunt me!)

'Yes, but how can you know?' the woman asked, shaking her head. She looked sad.

'Mmmm,' I agreed vaguely. I knew the reality of the dairy and egg industries probably wasn't nice, but I'd avoided looking into them. I didn't want to see what happened to cows and chickens. I liked cows and chickens, but I loved cheese. Cheese wasn't just my favourite food – it was a lifelong love affair. I used to joke with my partner that if it were a choice between him and cheese it would be a case of, 'See ya later, mate – and pass the Parmesan on your way out.' I would demolish whole wheels of Brie, ball after ball of mozzarella, huge slabs of Cheddar, blocks of halloumi. When I went on holiday I packed Port-Salut. I was no cheese snob, either; if there was Babybel to be had, or even Cheestrings, I'd be on it. I couldn't imagine life without cheese. I didn't *want* to imagine life without it. What kind of life would that even be? I shuddered at the thought.

Still, I followed this woman on social media. I kept one eye on her activism, but I carried on eating cheese and milk and eggs, feeling relatively virtuous because I wasn't eating meat. Meat was the worst thing, wasn't it? That was the real evil. Dairy and eggs couldn't be as bad as meat. They just couldn't be.

I carried on eating animal products, but it was like a seed had been planted in my mind. I couldn't forget what that woman had said – 'Yes, but how can you know?' – and how sad she'd looked when she'd said it. I tried to bury the seed underneath other concerns – work and money and life and the future. These things were more important, anyway, weren't they? I had other things to think about. I knew, on some level, I was looking away from the truth – but I didn't want to face it.

Then, in May 2016, I quit my job to travel. After years of dreaming about escaping the confines of a nine-to-five job, I'd finally saved up enough to make it happen. It felt like the trip of a lifetime: 17 months on the road, visiting all those countries I'd daydreamed about at work when I should have been writing content that drove engagement. It felt like a new beginning. I was brimming with excitement.

You'll probably come back a whole new person, people told me. Trips like these change you, I heard. This will be the making of you. *Would it?* I just wanted to have fun and see the world. I wanted to sip piña coladas on beaches, I wanted to explore ancient Mayan temples. I wanted to ride mopeds through exotic cities, to get lost in maze-like markets. And I wanted to eat – a lot.

Trying new food (and drink) was definitely the thing my partner Tom and I were most excited about. Tacos in Mexico! Arepas in Colombia! Banh mi in Vietnam! Curry in Cambodia! Wine in Chile…and Argentina…and New Zealand! Other than growing 17 months older, I didn't think this trip would really change me. I wasn't going to 'find myself'. I was going for the fun and the food.

And it was the trip of a lifetime – but it wasn't until I'd been travelling for almost a year and a half that my real journey began.

During my trip, there were multiple experiences that made me think about the way we, as a species, treat animals. I knew I was against animal cruelty – isn't everyone? – but how strongly was I against it? To what degree was I prepared to turn a blind eye? Was it only when it benefited me and my taste buds? If so, how did I feel about that?

In Nicaraguan markets I walked past lizards tied by rope, waiting silently, patiently, to be bought and killed. In New Zealand I watched as wide-eyed lambs were led into trucks that would take them to the slaughterhouse, gazing back at me on their final journey. In Thailand I saw wriggling fish being hacked into pieces like they were inanimate objects.

I USED TO SAY VEGANISM IS THE FUTURE, BUT I DON'T SAY THAT ANY MORE – VEGANISM IS NOW

In Vietnam I saw birds confined to tiny cages, unable to stretch their delicate wings. When I saw these things I felt desperately sad, and the seed in my mind grew a little more.

And then, in Bali, in June 2017, I spent two weeks in the town of Ubud. This was where I discovered just how good vegan food could be. I ate velvety cheesecakes and creamy lasagnes, exclaiming, 'What's in this? How are they doing this without dairy?' I'd had no idea plant-based food could be rich and decadent. I'd thought it was all salads and lentils and couscous. I'd always assumed I was too much of a foodie to be vegan, but maybe it was time to start thinking a bit more about this.

And then one day, I saw a van drive into a square. 'Don't look,' Tom said – so of course I did. In the back of the van were about fifty chickens, and as I looked closer I saw that half of them were already dead. The rest were barely alive, and I stared in horror. I remember this so well, and even now it makes me sad: the chickens' wings were bent at awful, odd angles, and their necks drooped onto their scrawny chests. Their heads knocked as the van jostled onto the pavement. I'd never thought chickens could look sad before, but these ones did – not just sad but forlorn, scared, tired and weak. The van reeked of urine. I'd never really thought about the journey animals go on to be killed before.

I'd never considered that the journey itself would be stressful and painful and scary. It simply hadn't entered my brain.

A man got out and began sweeping the chickens onto trays as if they meant nothing. He started carrying them away, the still-alive chickens jostling against the dead bodies. I couldn't look any more, and I turned away as tears filled my eyes.

Were those chickens meat-chickens or eggs-chickens, I wondered. I was trying to absolve myself; if they were for meat, I wasn't culpable, was I? I couldn't be blamed. I didn't eat meat. It wasn't my fault.

I was deeply upset by what I'd seen, but again, I tried to push it from my mind. I was thinking more and more about veganism, but I wasn't ready to make that commitment yet. No more cheese, no more eggs; what would I eat for breakfast?

I tried not to think about it too much, but another seed had been planted in my mind – and this time it wouldn't go. It lodged itself at the front of my brain and began to grow.

'When we get home I think I'm going to go almost-vegan,' I told Tom. 'But if I want an occasional cheeseboard as a treat, I'll have that. So like 99 per cent vegan.' We were heading home in September, so that would surely be the time to make the switch. No one *goes* vegan while travelling, do they? People thought I wouldn't find enough things to eat as a vegetarian (I gained 14 pounds while travelling so they needn't have worried!).

But even though we still had a month left, I found I couldn't look away any more. One evening, while I was reviewing a hotel in Abu Dhabi, I went down a rabbit hole. First, I watched a speech by animal activist Gary Yourofsky on YouTube. Afterwards, I sat in silence, shaken, trying to process what I'd seen and heard. It was a genuine lightbulb moment; I couldn't believe I'd never questioned myself before this. Not *seriously* questioned. How could I have squealed in delight over calves but looked away from what happens to them so I could eat dairy? How could I have cooed

The rise of veganism is unstoppable and momentum is building like a snowball.

over yellow chicks but not faced up to their fate because I liked scrambled eggs? How could I not have made the connection?

My mind was, finally, made up. I was going vegan – now, and full vegan. No piece of cheese would ever pass my lips again – and to the best of my knowledge it hasn't. But I needed more motivation, more conviction, more facts, more truth. I stayed up most of the night watching documentaries and YouTube videos, and then, at 5am, I dragged myself to bed, my mind still spinning. Just before I drifted off to sleep I remembered we'd hung our breakfast order outside our door – shakshuka, a Middle Eastern dish of tomatoes, onions and poached eggs. But no eggs would be eaten on my watch. I brought the order into our room and tore it in half. Knowing Tom would wake before me, I left a note for him: 'I'm vegan now,' it read. 'I've cancelled breakfast. You can go down and eat at the buffet.'

And that was that. Kind of.

Because I was already a vegetarian, I didn't think the switch to veganism would be drastic. I never expected it to have such an acute effect on the way I viewed the world. But it changed everything, and in a good way. Going vegan has, without a flicker of doubt, been the best decision of my life. I'm not alone in thinking this – ask a vegan what their biggest regret is and almost all will say not doing it sooner.

This is something Lewis Hamilton mused over before he made the switch: 'Every person I have ever met who has gone vegan says it is the best decision they have ever made.' It's true – but why does it affect us like this? How can giving up the things we love bring so much pleasure?

We'll get to that soon.

I'm not going to pretend that going vegan hasn't come without adversity. At times it's caused me to feel pain, shock and deep sadness. It's made me swell with anger, frustration and bitterness. But so much more often, it's filled me with joy. It's made me feel a sense of positivity and power. It's flooded me with excitement, with a feeling of forward momentum – like I'm doing something that matters. It makes me happy, something I would have laughed at before: *How could giving up cheese make me happy?*

Like many people, when I thought about going vegan, I'd focused on everything I thought I'd miss. I didn't know what I would gain. Aside from the health benefits, which we'll explore later, and the knowledge that you're doing the single biggest thing anyone can to reduce their impact on the earth, there's another, more intrinsic benefit – one I had no idea even existed until I made the change. One that actually inspired this book, because I wanted to share it with people. I wanted people to know how rewarding veganism is. Being vegan isn't some

IF YOU KILL
A PIG, YOU'RE
NORMAL.
IF YOU KILL
A DOG,
YOU'RE SICK.

IF YOU
KILL
NEITHER,
THEN
YOU'RE AN
EXTREMIST.

sacrificial act that might be morally sound but is also restrictive and dull. In fact it's fun and exciting and gratifying.

But as with most things worth having, getting the reward and reaping the benefits doesn't come without work, and my first year of being vegan was definitely a learning curve.

The Reaction

When I confronted the realities of animal agriculture and became aware of the effect it had on the environment, like a lot of new vegans I was filled with outrage. *What's happening to our planet? What's happening to these animals? How is this legal? Why won't people look?*

It was overwhelming. I was filled with this burning need to tell people the truth. Never mind that nobody wanted to listen – I was on a mission. I knew the people around me were good people, kind people. They didn't *want* to harm animals. They all wanted to protect our planet. Yet they were unwittingly paying for animals to be abused and killed, for our world to be destroyed. If I had known the full facts, I thought, I would have made the change sooner. If someone had shown me that footage and told me the truth, I would have listened, and I would have changed. So why weren't the people around me listening and changing?

There was something else I found hard to understand that first year. It concerned people's reactions to veganism. When I told people that I was going vegan, few people had a positive response. One of my best friends said, when I told her, 'Oh not another one! I'm going to have cull you!' She was joking, of course, and her reaction certainly wasn't unique, but I wondered what it was about not wanting to eat animals, or the things that come out of them, that gets people's backs up.

Some reactions I got were doubtful, some were sceptical. Others varied from defensive and aggressive to outright scorn and ridicule. Just saying the words 'I'm vegan' in reply to something – because it was relevant – elicited the strangest responses. Some people felt the need to tell me how much they loved bacon. Others would say how they could never in a million years go vegan (pretty much every vegan has said that at some point, for the record!). Some people told me that they didn't eat much meat at all, and the meat they did buy – very infrequently – was the really good stuff from the nice humane farm down the road where the animals had the best life and were totally happy to be killed.

Thankfully, as time has passed, the reactions to veganism have become much more positive. These days, you're more likely to hear, 'Wow, good for you!' than 'Er, *why*?' if you tell people you're going vegan – one of the many markers of how far this movement has come in just a few years. But I find it fascinating to examine how people react to veganism. According to The Vegan Society, by definition, it's just 'a way of living which seeks to exclude, as far as is possible and practicable, all forms of exploitation of, and cruelty to, animals.' Is that something to get annoyed at?

There are reasons why some people find vegans annoying. They think we're virtuous. Smug. Militant. Aggressive. Judgemental. Tedious. Obsessive. Protein-deficient. Unwashed. I could go on. When I appeared on breakfast television I was branded – along with every other vegan on the planet – 'sanctimonious'. There are millions of vegans in the world and

Humans are dying of starvation, but farmed animals never miss a meal.

we're *all* sanctimonious. Honestly, that's quite the achievement.

'Extreme' is another trait vegans are branded with. This one has always seemed strange to me – because we're all against animal cruelty, aren't we? Most of us admit we probably couldn't kill an animal ourselves. We're outraged by the Yulin Dog Meat Festival in China, appalled when poachers shoot a lion or a giraffe. When people hurt a dog or cat we scream bloody murder. But we pick and choose what counts as cruelty based on the species of the animal and the context of the cruelty. The thinking seems to be: if you kill a pig, you're normal. If you kill a dog, you're sick. If you kill neither, then you're an extremist. Animal cruelty is a terrible thing, but cows, pigs, sheep, chickens? They aren't victims. They don't count.

During the first few months of being vegan, I was repeatedly struck by how inconsistent we are as a society, and there was one story I read in particular that stayed with me. In 2015 a man in Florida deliberately ran over nine ducklings with a lawnmower. Online, people were outraged, and I spent a while reading comments. The internet thought this man was 'sick'. He was a 'low-life monster'. A 'special place in hell' awaited him. The man pled guilty to animal cruelty and was sentenced to a year in prison, but that wasn't enough. He deserved the same treatment, people thought – to be run over with a lawnmower, or maybe thrown off a building. One commenter thought the sentence was harsh – it was 'just some ducklings', after all – and someone responded that 'the ducklings were living and breathing animals that did not deserve to be murdered like this.'

I remember, quite clearly, thinking how mad this all was. How nothing made sense any more. In the egg industry, it's standard procedure to kill male chicks. They're considered worthless because they don't lay eggs, and so every year, around seven billion male chicks are killed.[1] Most are macerated in high-speed grinders: day-old chicks are sent along conveyor belts and tipped into grinding machines where they're minced up alive. The UK alone kills thirty to forty million newborn chicks each year.[2] All of these chicks were also 'living and breathing animals that did not deserve to be murdered like this.' But where is the outrage?

I couldn't stop comparing the duckling incident – an anomaly, a story so shocking it was reported around the world – to what happens to millions of chicks every day. What was the difference? How can we be incensed by one but be apathetic about the other? It was bizarre, seeing people who classed themselves as animal lovers get angry when other people just didn't want to eat animals.

THEY THINK WE'RE VIRTUOUS. SMUG. MILITANT. AGGRESSIVE. JUDGEMENTAL. TEDIOUS. OBSESSIVE. PROTEIN-DEFICIENT. UNWASHED.

I couldn't understand how our society could be so contradictory.

But there are, in fact, powerful, deep-rooted reasons why people react like this, and in order to make sense of it all, I had to do some research.

The Reasoning

The term I was looking for, in my quest to understand, was cognitive dissonance. It describes the discomfort experienced by someone who performs actions that conflict with their beliefs or values. It can be so unsettling for us to face the fact that we're doing things we don't agree with, that we go to extreme lengths to justify our actions and alleviate our feelings of guilt – feelings that sometimes we're not even aware we feel. This concept is so common when it comes to eating animals that there's a specific term for it: the meat paradox.

When I spoke to people about veganism, time and again I came across this paradox. We don't want to make the connection between the foods we eat and the living being from which it came – and in a world where the reality of farms and slaughterhouses is hidden from us, it's easy to do. We laugh at people instead of listening – because it's easier – and, to defend our behaviour, we assign animals ranks: pets, wild animals or animals that are food. We tell ourselves they exist for that reason – so we can eat them.

The meat paradox also describes how we minimize the intellectual and emotional capabilities of the animals we eat. We deny them their consciousness: they can't think or reason, so they can't suffer. Science tells us that animals feel emotions – including joy and shame, jealousy and grief, love and rage – but we don't want to think that the animals we eat feel these. Pigs are more intelligent than dogs, but we don't want to think that our bacon was smarter than our pets. Accepting that causes our brains to panic, so we tell ourselves that we need to eat animal protein for our health. It's part of our culture and history. These animals had a good life. And man, it just tastes too damn good.

These contradictions are all around us. People say eating meat is natural, yet most people go to great lengths to distance themselves from the fact that what they're eating was an animal who lived and breathed and thought and felt. We disconnect the food from the animal. We reduce a once-living being to a chunk of meat. We eat in denial.

On Reddit not so long ago, people were up in arms because someone took a photo of the pork belly they ordered, and there was still a nipple attached. People were disgusted. It was 'gross'. It made them 'want to vomit'. We're literally eating the belly of a once-living mammal, yet we can't bear to be reminded of that. Sure, we know it on an intellectual level, the same way we know when we're eating meat that an animal had to die, but we do everything we can to not really confront that. 'I try to not think of my meat as being living before,' one person wrote. 'Oh Jesus,' another commented. 'See, I don't see an animal when I eat meat, but then you show me things like this and I start to believe it really is an animal.'

It's true that some people don't feel discomfort at the idea of an animal suffering or being killed for their benefit. But these people are the minority. I've had a lot of people – friends and strangers – say things to me like, 'I love eating animals!' or 'I'm totally fine with cows dying for my burger.' But in most cases, this is a defence mechanism. It's one thing to *say* you're fine with what happens, and quite another to actually be so. Every person to whom I've shown slaughterhouse footage has been deeply upset or disturbed. Lack of empathy for animals is a major cause for concern in children, and for good reason. Perhaps, if you're a farmer or a hunter, you get used to what happens, but most of us are disconnected from the reality of animal slaughter. We're shielded from the truth, and when we see it, it shocks and it hurts.

In order to eat the things we like, we disengage and disconnect. Pig becomes pork, cow becomes beef.

We create distance between the meat and the animal. Pigs can think and feel and suffer, pork cannot. It's the reason people are squeamish about eating fish with the face attached, or chicken when the head hasn't been removed. It's the reason the word 'harvested' is now used in the USA instead of 'killed' or 'slaughtered'.

Understanding these thought processes helped me change the way I viewed and talked about veganism in two ways. Firstly, it helped me understand precisely *why* going vegan feels like such a profound and positive thing to do. Before, I'd struggled to describe to people just how good it felt; to adequately convey the joys of plant-based living. But understanding how our minds work helped me put a nail on it, to grasp why it felt so freeing.

Pigs are more intelligent than dogs, but we don't want to think that our bacon was smarter than our pets.

Because most of us don't want to think that what we're eating once had a heartbeat, we use techniques like denial and distancing. It works – but it comes at a price. We do things we can't face up to. We turn away from violence and bloodshed. We ignore the suffering of animals – animals we'd try to save and protect in any other situation. When you go vegan, that guilt and discomfort dissipates, and what you gain in its place is a feeling of empowerment and liberation. When you align your actions with your ethics there's no inner conflict. There's no inconsistencies, no denial. You feel like yourself – like a better version of yourself.

You're choosing to live your life without ever intentionally hurting other living beings. Choosing to see an animal as 'someone', not 'something'. Choosing to be kinder to our planet, kinder to your body and your mind. When you choose to live kindly, every day feels like an opportunity. Every mealtime becomes a joy. You're choosing to evolve, to move forward with the times. We're not cavemen any more – so why are we still eating like them?

Extending the Circle

The second way that exploring cognitive dissonance and the meat paradox helped me was by allowing me to feel empathy for the people who argued

EMBRACING VEGANISM ISN'T MERELY ABOUT ADOPTING A NEW WAY OF EATING AND LIVING, IT'S ABOUT LETTING GO OF AN OLD ONE – ONE THAT BROUGHT US COMFORT AND HAPPINESS.

against veganism. I recognized how unsettling it was to question whether something we've done all our lives, without thinking, might be unnecessary – or worse, cruel. It's so much easier to believe we really do need animal protein to be healthy; that it is natural, part of the food chain; that these animals aren't really suffering. And I remembered then, with some shame, how I'd watched those poor chickens arrive in trucks in Bali, dead and dying, and how it had made me cry – but how I still hadn't gone vegan. Who was I to judge?

When people pushed back against veganism, I could appreciate what an emotive subject it was. It wasn't that people didn't want to stop animals' pain or support a more sustainable way of living, it was that our eating habits sit deep in our culture and memory. They're part of us, and that makes it hard to let go. It isn't just about the food itself, it's what we associate with it: egg and soldiers before school, chicken soup when you're sick, roast beef on a Sunday afternoon. Embracing veganism isn't merely about adopting a new way of eating and living, it's about letting go of an old one – one that brought us comfort and happiness.

If compassion was something I was advocating, then I had to show that. I had to extend my circle of empathy past animals and onto people, too.

The 'divide' between vegans and non-vegans can seem vast, but I don't think it is, really. If we scratch beneath the surface, most people share the same beliefs and values. We're against animal cruelty. We don't believe animals should suffer unnecessarily. Most of us are already on the same page, psychologically. It's just that our actions don't always reflect what we truly believe.

Empathy is so important – because without it there can be no affinity between vegans and non-vegans, no meaningful conversation. When people feel attacked, they get defensive, and this widens the chasm, the sense of 'us and them'. If we want people to think about their actions, they need to feel secure doing so. Having conversations about veganism shouldn't be about attacking people for making bad choices – it should about encouraging them to make better ones.

Now, when someone tells me they don't agree with veganism, I usually just explain what it really means – because one thing I've learned over the past few years is that a lot of people don't actually know. Veganism is not a pursuit of perfection. It's not a way to elevate yourself or show your superiority. It's not a way to annoy the people around you. It's just about minimizing harm – to animals and to our environment. No one's ever scoffed at that or said it sounds extreme, and that's because, when it's communicated rationally and reasonably, most people can see this way of living makes sense – even if they continue to make the same choices out of habit or convenience, or even apathy.

The time to change is now. History is unfolding, now. The rise of veganism is unstoppable and momentum is building like a snowball. You can see the change on the street, in restaurants, online. American business magnate Bill Gates has pumped one billion dollars into the plant-based food company Beyond Meat. Lab-grown meat is set to make the world's largest industry obsolete. There are vegan burgers in McDonald's, Burger King, KFC. We're behind enemy lines, and the infiltration won't stop. Vegans won't stop, because the price is too high.

More than seventy billion land animals are killed every single year – for a sandwich. We are in the midst of an environmental crisis that's driven by meat and dairy. Humans are dying of starvation, but farmed animals never miss a meal. The world's leading scientists are united on two things: that we need to change the way we eat; and that time is running out.

Now, we have a choice. We can take the biggest step possible to ensure our children and grandchildren have a future – that they inherit a world where there are fish in the ocean and animals on the land. We can choose to never intentionally harm another living being – to live more kindly, more sustainably, more in tune with our planet and the other creatures on it.

Or we can do nothing.

We can choose not to take that step. We can remain apathetic while our planet dies, while animals die. We can continue to eat like ancient man did, as if our world hasn't changed.

But our world has changed. It's evolved, and it's time for us to evolve with it. Let's take that step. Let's make that choice – and let's get on the right side of history, before it's too late.

I used to say veganism is the future, but I don't say that any more. Veganism is now.

THE FACTS

Veganism is rising at an unprecedented rate. Research shows that in the UK, the number of vegans has increased 360 per cent over the past decade[1]; the USA saw a 600 per cent increase in just three years.[2] Before we look at *how* to go vegan, let's look at why so many people are making this change.

Studies show there are three main causes for the rise in veganism: concern about the environment, animals and health. These are three very different catalysts – with powerful reasoning behind them.

As much as I want this book to be positive and fun, some of the information in this section makes for pretty grim reading. But facts are important, and knowledge is power. We do need to know the truth to know how we feel, so that not only can we make informed decisions, but actually own our decisions, too.

Let's take a closer look at the facts.

The Environment

Make no bones about it, we are in the midst of a global crisis. The years from 2014–19 have been the hottest on record.[1] Levels of carbon dioxide in the atmosphere are up 46 per cent.[2] Eight million metric tons of plastic enter our oceans each year.[3] Every day eighty thousand acres of rainforest are destroyed.[4] Back in 2018, the world's leading climate scientists warned that we have just 12 years before the world we know is lost forever. Time is running out – fast.

As a society, we've never been more environmentally conscious than now. Most of us recycle. We shop with reusable bags. We wouldn't dream of using plastic straws. But despite decades of warnings about the damage we're doing to our planet, we've dragged our heels when it comes to making the changes that make the most difference.

Animal agriculture is the leading cause of species extinction, ocean dead zones, water pollution and habitat destruction. According to a comprehensive study in 2018 on the effect of farming on our environment, led by researchers at Oxford University, adopting a plant-based diet is probably 'the single biggest way to reduce your impact on planet Earth.'[5] Its overall impact is greater than reducing the number of flights you take or buying an electric car, the study found, because these steps only cut back on greenhouse gas emissions. Conversely, a vegan diet slashes not only greenhouse gases, but also global acidification (a decrease in the pH of earth's oceans due to carbon dioxide in the atmosphere), eutrophication (an excessive build-up of nutrients in rivers, lakes and the sea), land use and water use.

'Agriculture is a sector that spans all the multitude of environmental problems,' lead researcher at Oxford University Joseph Poore stated. 'Really it is animal products that are responsible for so much of this. Avoiding consumption of animal products delivers far better environmental benefits than trying to purchase sustainable meat and dairy.'

When so much emphasis is placed on turning lights off and walking instead of driving, I know the role animal agriculture plays in environmental devastation can sound shocking – and maybe rather unbelievable. It's easy to see how things such as fracking and fumes do damage – but a slice of ham, a hunk of cheese? Are they *really* that bad?

Well, yes. The more we've learned over the years, the more clear it is: animal agriculture is destroying our planet at an utterly uncontrollable rate.

So let's break this down.

Land Use

- Livestock covers 45 per cent of all land on earth.[6]
- 83 per cent of the world's farmland is used to rear livestock.[7]

- One-third of all rangeland on our planet is desertified, with animal agriculture being the main driving force.[8]
- A meat-eating diet requires 18 times more land than a vegan diet.[9]

The Oxford University study summarized the results from 570 smaller studies. These studies took their findings from around 40,000 farms in 119 countries, looking at 40 different food products and considering the total environmental impact each product had. The research shows that, without meat and dairy, we could reduce our use of farmland by more than 75 per cent[10] and still comfortably feed the world. The size of the area we would get back? About the same as the USA, Australia, China and the EU combined.

Every minute, seven football fields' worth of Amazon forest is bulldozed to clear more room for livestock.[11] The leading cause of species extinction, of one-third of all rangeland being desertified and of rainforest destruction is making room for livestock and their feed crops.

Ultimately, using land to grow plants for animals to eat is just plain inefficient. A meat-eater requires 18 times more land than a vegan simply because, on a plant-based diet, plants are eaten directly, rather than being grown and fed to animals so that we can then eat the animals.

THE CONCEPT OF FISHLESS OCEANS ONCE SEEMED IMPOSSIBLE – NOW IT'S A LIKELY REALITY FOR OUR CHILDREN

Oceans

- Fishless oceans could be a reality by 2048.[12]
- Up to 2.7 trillion animals are pulled from our oceans every year.[13]
- Only three per cent of the world's oceans are free from human pressure.[14]
- The leading cause of plastic in the ocean is abandoned fishing gear.[15]

Once a sanctuary, large parts of oceans today are wastelands. Ocean dead zones – areas where marine life can't survive due to low oxygen levels – have quadrupled in size since 1950[16], and waste pollution from animal agriculture is a leading cause. The meat industry was specifically blamed for creating a dead zone in the Gulf of Mexico that was larger than New Jersey. A report showed that toxic runoff from manure and fertilizer had poured into the ocean, causing a lack of oxygen that destroyed marine life.[17] When oceans are depleted of oxygen, fish either die or flee, and plants, slow-moving animals and shellfish slowly suffocate.

Then there's the direct effect of fishing. Up to forty per cent of fish and marine animals caught globally are discarded as bycatch[18], and larger marine animals such as sharks, dolphins, whales and tuna are especially susceptible. Scientists estimate that approximately 650,000 whales, dolphins and seals were killed each year during the 1990s by fishing boats.[19] Sharks fare much worse: around forty to fifty million are killed each year in fishing lines and nets.[20]

The concept of fishless oceans once seemed impossible – now it's a likely reality for our children.

Campaigns to ban plastic straws are useful for inspiring awareness, but the leading cause of plastic in the ocean is abandoned fishing gear – 'ghost gear'. According to a 2018 report from World Animal Protection, ghost gear is 'the most harmful form of marine debris'[21], killing millions of animals each year. Nearly half the weight of the 'Great Pacific Garbage Patch' – a drifting stretch of rubbish twice the size of France, weighing 79,000 metric tons – is fishing nets, with the majority of the rest composed of other fishing gear.[22]

For all our talk about reducing single-use plastic to protect our oceans, the main cause of it is rarely acknowledged, let alone tackled. There is a sad, strange dichotomy in declining a plastic straw to 'save the oceans' and then tucking into a plate of sushi without a thought.

Water Supply

- ◆ 3,000 litres (660 gallons) of water is required to produce one hamburger[23] – equivalent to two months' worth of showers for the average Westerner.

- 2,030 litres (477 gallons) of water are needed to produce 450g (1lb) of eggs; it's nearly double that for cheese.[24]
- 11,197 litres (2,463 gallons) of water are needed to produce 450g (1lb) of beef; for the same amount of tofu, it's 995 litres (219 gallons).[25]

Water might cover most of our planet, but we shouldn't make the mistake of thinking the world can't run out of drinkable water. According to a NASA study, many of our freshwater sources are being depleted faster than they are being replenished.[26]

In the USA alone, 56 per cent of water is used to grow crops that are fed to animals.[27] But animals need to drink as well as eat, and cows and pigs can drink a *lot*. Humans drink nearly 20 billion

Every day, as the tropical rainforest is destroyed, up to 135 plant, animal and insect species are lost forever.

litres (4.4 billion gallons) of water a day; cows bred for meat and dairy drink about eight-and-a-half times that amount. Globally, animal agriculture is responsible for up to 33 per cent of all freshwater consumption[28] – that's one-third of all drinkable water.

The problem doesn't just relate to water use, though – it's also related to what we're putting *in* the water – which is, frankly, a whole load of crap. In the USA, livestock produce more than ten times more waste[29] than the entire population: the Environmental Protection Agency estimates that around 335 million tons of manure is produced each year. In the words of Jeff Goldblum in *Jurassic Park* (1993), 'Now that is one big pile of shit.'

While this waste is meant to be contained safely, storm damage or incorrect storage can cause it to be released into waterways. When the waste decomposes it releases nutrients, pathogens and ammonia, which pollute the water and cause mass fish die-offs. But this type of pollution doesn't just harm the natural environment. Animal waste can contain more than a hundred pathogens causing human diseases[30], and can also contain metals, such as lead, that cause kidney issues and nervous system disorders. People working on or near pig farms have a higher risk of several diseases of the airways, including asthma.

A plant-based diet reduces not only the amount

of water waste, but also how much waste goes into the water.

Animals and the Environment

- More than seventy billion land animals are slaughtered for food each year.[31]
- Industrial farming is driving the sixth mass extinction of life on Earth.[32]
- Globally, 28,000 species are threatened with extinction – 27 per cent of all assessed species.[33]

In 2019 an extensive report by the United Nations (UN)[34] brought home the damage we've done to our planet. Nature is declining at a speed never seen before, and 70 per cent of agriculture is now related to meat production. Our growing demands for more meat, more fish, more cheese are causing a total biodiversity collapse that's driving the sixth mass extinction of life on earth. The second biggest cause of this extinction? Hunting and killing animals for food: three hundred species are currently being eaten into extinction.

In 2018 a major study by the World Wildlife Fund (WWF)[35] found that the UK's food supply was linked to the extinction of an estimated 33 species. If we continue the way we are, giant pandas, snow leopards, cheetahs, giraffes and jaguars could all soon be extinct. Gorillas, lions, forest elephants, chimpanzees, hippos and some species of dolphin are already teetering on

IT TAKES MORE THAN 31 YEARS FOR A BILLION SECONDS TO TICK BY.

WE KILL MORE THAN A BILLION ANIMALS EVERY SIX DAYS.

the brink of extinction. This is before we even begin to think about the thousands of plant, marine and insect species that are less publicly recognized.

The key cause of species extinction is the destruction of natural habitats to create farmland. Our unbridled consumption of food doesn't just threaten animals, the world's leading experts have warned, but our very existence. Our need for clean air and water now hang in the balance. 'We are sleepwalking towards the edge of a cliff,' the executive director of science and conservation at the WWF said. Is there another way to put it? We are literally destroying our entire ecosystem for the sake of a cheeseburger.

Greenhouse Gases

- Animal agriculture produces more greenhouse gases than all transportation combined.[36]
- Meat, eggs and dairy provide just 18 per cent of global calories and 37 per cent of global protein, yet produce 60 per cent of agriculture's greenhouse gas emissions.[37]

Farming systems differ around the world, so it's hard to determine the exact scale of greenhouse gas emissions from animal agriculture – but, due to the prevalence of crude oil in farming and the flatulent nature of livestock, we know that it's a lot.

A comprehensive study by the UN found that raising livestock for meat, eggs and milk generates 18 per cent of global greenhouse gas emissions[38]. This is more than the combined exhaust of all transportation – more than every car, truck, bus, ship, plane and rocket combined.

Another study found that 'the world's top five meat and dairy corporations are now responsible for more annual greenhouse gas emissions than Exxon, Shell or BP.'[39] The report went on to state that while the oil industry is generally blamed for its massive, toxic contribution to global warming, the meat and dairy industries face very little scrutiny and should be held accountable for the harm they cause. More needs to be done, the report concluded, to educate the public on the impact of animal agriculture.

Deforestation

→ Animal agriculture is responsible for up to 91 per cent of the destruction in the Amazon.[40]

→ Up to 135 plant, animal and insect species are lost every day due to rainforest destruction.[41]

→ Between 1990 and 2016, the world lost 502,000 square miles (1.3 million square km) of forest – an area larger than South Africa.[42]

Our demand for meat is so big that we ran out of land a long time ago. To clear space for livestock and to

OUR NEED FOR CLEAN AIR AND WATER NOW HANG IN THE BALANCE.

grow the vast amount of crops they need, we began destroying the rainforest. Because burning trees is cheaper than chopping them, many companies simply razed huge stretches to the ground. When centuries-old trees are burned, huge amounts of carbon dioxide are released into the air.

Since 1970, more than ninety per cent of all Amazon deforestation has occurred to clear land for grazing livestock[43], and aside from the land needed for the animals themselves, large swathes of what was once rainforest are now soya plantations. Critics of veganism often argue that soya is unsustainable, yet the overwhelming majority of it is used for animal feed. Only six per cent of all soya is used for human consumption[44] – and most of that is grown in the USA.

The rate of this destruction is hard to grasp. Exact numbers remain somewhat elusive, but experts agree that every day we lose at least 80,000 acres

(32,375 hectares) of tropical rainforest – and a further 80,000 acres (32,375 hectares) is simultaneously harmed. Every day, as the tropical rainforest is destroyed, up to 135 plant, animal and insect species are lost forever.

These ancient rainforests are home to more than half of the world's animal species. More than a quarter of modern medicine comes partly from rainforests, but less than one per cent of rainforest plants have actually been tested. Rainforests are a medicinal treasure trove waiting to be discovered, but as we burn them to sow soya to fatten cows, their wonders will go uncharted.

Away from the Amazon, the once-great rainforests of Sumatra and Borneo have been flattened, mainly to produce palm oil. The prevalence of palm oil in food and cosmetics is well known – but palm kernel meal, a by-product of palm oil, is also used in animal feed. More than a tenth of all palm kernel meal is fed to pets and livestock in the UK.[45]

The Animals

Since going vegan, I've learned that it's the topic of animals that's the most contentious. Easily. Almost everyone agrees we need to eat less meat to protect the environment, but the issue of animals, and personal ethics, is a whole different ball game.

Talking about animals and what happens to them is usually what gets vegans accused of 'preaching'. It's when tempers are most likely to run high – on both sides.

For many people, killing animals is already a provocative issue, so while I'm not going to sugarcoat this section, I'm also not going to embellish or use overly emotive language when I'm describing standard farming procedures. We just need to know the reality of what happens to animals in order for us to eat meat, fish, dairy and eggs.

Before we look into the reality of animal agriculture, it's important to cover two points. We have already looked at cognitive dissonance and the meat paradox, exploring how, often unconsciously, we try to justify what we do to animals. One way we do this is by denying animals their consciousness. The other is by convincing ourselves the animals had wonderful lives and didn't suffer. When I speak to people about the reality of farming and what animals experience, these two issues come up all the time, so before we go any further, let's address them.

The Issue of Consciousness

For years, debate has raged around whether or not animals are conscious. But what do we actually mean by consciousness?

In animals, essentially it just means they're sentient: they experience what happens to them in real time, they feel emotions, they have a sense of purpose, they experience varying mental states. Anyone who's ever known a dog will have no problem agreeing that animals are conscious and sentient, but it's something that's been denied for a long time. If animals aren't conscious, the argument seemed to be, then what does it matter if they suffer?

In 2012 a group of prominent scientists, including Stephen Hawking – all experts in the fields of neuroscience and animal cognition – signed something called the Cambridge Declaration on Consciousness. This declaration stated that 'animals have the neuroanatomical, neurochemical, and neurophysiological substrates of conscious states along with the capacity to exhibit intentional behaviours. Consequently, the weight of evidence indicates that humans are not unique in possessing the neurological substrates that generate consciousness. Non-human animals, including all mammals and birds, and many other creatures, including octopuses, also possess these neurological substrates.'

Or, in plain language – animals are conscious in the same way that humans are. This doesn't mean they're as intelligent as we are, but they're conscious, sentient beings all the same. Like us,

THERE IS
NO WAY TO
HUMANELY KILL
A LIVING BEING
WHO DOESN'T
WANT TO DIE

they're invested in their lives. They want to live. They seek pleasure. They avoid suffering. They feel grief, rage, confusion, joy.

Back in 1789 British philosopher Jeremy Bentham asked a question about animals that's even more relevant today: 'The question is not "Can they reason?",' he asked, 'Nor "Can they talk?" but "Can they suffer?".'

In my mind, this is the question that truly matters. I think we can agree that the answer is yes. So now, let's ask another question. If we don't need to kill to survive, can we morally justify killing an animal who doesn't want to die?

The Myth of 'Humane' Meat

We are, on the whole, animal lovers. Because we don't want to harm animals and we take no pleasure from their pain, we want to believe that the meat, dairy, fish and eggs we buy come from animals who live happy, fulfilling lives. We want to believe they died without suffering, without pain – without even knowing what hit them.

But, sadly, this isn't true. What we need to remember is that the meat, dairy and egg industries are some of the most powerful in the world. These companies spend vast amounts of money hiding the truth from us. They conceal the reality of slaughter, and they manipulate well-intentioned consumers into thinking they're buying high-welfare products. The majority of people I speak to are utterly convinced they buy high-welfare, 'ethical' meat – but in the UK, 94 per cent of chicken sold is intensively farmed. In the USA, 99 per cent of all meat is factory farmed.

The reason most of us mistakenly believe we're buying high-welfare animal products is because we're being misled. Labels such as 'happy eggs' and 'humane meat' are marketing myths, calculated ploys that exist only to make us feel better, to alleviate any guilt we might be experiencing.

In the UK, 85 per cent of pig farms are certified to have 'high-welfare' standards – but the majority of UK pork comes from intensive operations where pigs live lives of utter misery. Investigations into these farms continually reveal shocking cruelty: undercover footage shows workers swinging piglets by their back legs and smashing their heads against the wall; pigs being shocked repeatedly with electric prods; the rotting bodies of dead piglets littering the floor; pigs living in cramped conditions, one on top of the other, alongside their dead siblings.

Of course, it isn't just pigs. 'High-welfare' standards are perfectly illustrated by the recommended advice for 'euthanizing' unwanted lambs: 'Hold the animal by the back legs and swing it through an arc to hit the back of its head with considerable force against a solid object, e.g. a brick wall or metal stanchion."[1] So basically, in the UK, smashing a lamb's head in against the wall constitutes 'humane destruction.'

In the USA, things are much worse. In spite of labels insisting products are 'certified humane', not a single federal law exists to protect animals on factory farms.[2] Not one. The overwhelming majority of egg-laying hens never spread their wings. Pigs are confined in crates so small they can never turn around. Male chicks are ground up alive.

And even when countries do have regulations or laws, all too often they're ignored. Time and again, footage recorded by animal activists all over the world shows shocking breaches of welfare laws. Undercover footage at an 'ethical', free-range farm in the UK revealed that 16,000 chickens were crammed inside a dark, narrow shed. Many of the chickens were bald, others were covered in mites, sores and wounds. A subsequent investigation found no breaches of regulation.

At dairy farms, covert investigations recorded workers abusing calves: dragging them by their legs, standing on them, force-feeding them, depriving them of water for 29 hours on one of the hottest days of the year. These incidents are by no means isolated.

The entire animal agriculture industry is shrouded in deception. Meat, dairy and egg packaging depicts animals living a blissful existence in the countryside, roaming free on sun-dappled farms – yet the only time many of these animals ever set foot outside or smell fresh air is on their final journey to the slaughterhouse. Supermarkets use fictitious farm names to sell their products: UK shoppers may be tempted by meat labelled with names like Willow Farms, Boswell Farms and Woodside Farms, but none of these farms actually exist. The illusion is given of small, cutesy, high-welfare farms, but it's just that – an illusion.

Even 'official' labelling is deceptive. 'Outdoor-bred' pork comes from pigs born to sows who live outdoors, but the piglets only spend four weeks outside before moving indoors for the next 16 weeks to be fattened up.

To be classed as free range, chickens only need a space the size of an iPad; 16,000 birds in one dingy shed counts as free range.

No matter where you live, the vast majority of meat we eat comes from animals who were confined indoors all their lives.

People truly believe they're buying high-welfare animal products, but they're being deceived – by the certification of the animal products, by language and labelling, by the packaging itself. It's only via undercover investigations that the brutal reality of farming has been exposed.

There are, of course, small, local farms where the standards are higher. But even there, it's a rose-tinted view of farming – one that skips conveniently past the reality of slaughter, the terrifying, often arduous journey the animals take to the abattoir. The truth is still hidden.

No matter how 'nicely' a farm may treat these animals, they all end up in the slaughterhouse, fighting for their lives. No matter how much farmers profess to care about their animals, the bottom line is that these animals exist for one reason only: so farmers can exploit their bodies for money. You can never have someone's best interests at heart when you're profiting from their death; when a living being becomes a commodity.

Between 2009 and 2017, animal rights group Animal Aid filmed inside 13 randomly selected UK slaughterhouses: 12 of them broke animal welfare laws. The resulting footage was so brutal and graphic it led to a law being passed mandating CCTV in all UK slaughterhouses. But despite this, the abuse continues – and if you doubt that, watch the footage.

'Ethical meat' and 'humane slaughter' are oxymorons. They cannot exist. These words mean compassion, benevolence, kindness – and because they mean this, the meat, dairy and egg industries can't be considered either ethical or humane. The end result of these industries is always the death of the animals, whether they're killed for their flesh or because they're not producing enough milk or eggs. They all die violent deaths. Even if the slaughter is, mercifully, quick, that doesn't mean it isn't violent.

There is no way to humanely kill a living being who doesn't want to die. It's a marketing ploy, an advertising tagline. It's a myth. It's a lie. Please don't fall for it.

It's time to take a closer look at the reality of farming for different species.

Cows

Let's begin with dairy, because this is the industry that's the most misunderstood. I believe that the insidious nature of the dairy industry is why many people think veganism is extreme. They understand being vegetarian, because the cruelty in meat – or just the simple fact that an animal was killed – is overt, but in dairy, everything is hidden. Where's the harm in just milking an animal, people think, especially if they have good lives and aren't killed?

In order to produce milk, cows must first be pregnant. This is an obvious point, but one that's frequently never considered: many people seem to believe these animals just spontaneously lactate, and we're doing them a favour by siphoning off the surplus milk. 'Cows would die if we didn't milk them!' is something I've read, and heard, far too many times.

On most farms, cows are impregnated via artificial insemination. The apparatus used has the nickname 'rape rack'. After a pregnancy of just over nine months, the cow gives birth. Her calf will be taken from her, usually within the first 24 hours. Cows are maternal mammals, and a forced separation can be extremely traumatic; in one case in the USA, the police were called when concerned locals heard strange noises from a nearby dairy farm. After investigating, the police found the cries were from cows mourning the loss of their calves. According to the police, it happens every year. Multiple videos online show cows relentlessly chasing trucks that are driving their calves away, or fighting, always futilely, to stop their calf being torn from them. Studies have shown that the newborn calves suffer from separation anxiety, engaging in repetitive crying and sometimes declining food.

Female calves are bred to join the milking herd, and usually spend the first few months of life confined in a lonely hutch. Because calves can't be drinking up all the cows' milk that's now meant for humans, they're fed on milk replacement.

Because they don't produce milk and are often considered unfit for beef production, male calves are frequently deemed as worthless. Many are shot at birth, others will be reared as veal. The demand for veal is low in the UK (it's deemed cruel) so these calves are usually shipped to veal farms in European countries. These journeys last for days and are painful and stressful: young calves can't regulate their body temperature to cope with the extreme heat and cold of long journeys, and can suffer bruising and weight loss. After arriving at the veal farms, they live in bleak conditions, unable to graze or walk on the grass. The calves are housed in tiny hutches or in veal crates, which are now illegal in the UK but legal in the USA and the rest of Europe. After just a few months, they'll be slaughtered. Veal is a direct by-product of the dairy industry.

Cows are selectively bred to produce as much milk as possible, which puts their bodies through enormous strain and often leads to mastitis, a painful udder infection. Conditions vary greatly: some cows are allowed out to graze for six months of the year, while others aren't allowed out at all. These 'zero-grazing' farms, where cows are shut up in sheds all year round, are becoming increasingly common.

Whatever environment they live in, dairy cows have been turned into milk machines. Their life consists of insemination, pregnancy, having their calves being forcibly taken, and then months of relentless milking – again and again and again. This huge physical burden has led to diseases becoming rampant in the industry. Unable to roam, and with concrete under their hooves instead of grass, many cows become lame. These cows are called 'spent cows', and when their bodies finally give out, usually at around four or five years old, they're sent to the slaughterhouse for cheap beef.

It's important to note that no matter how 'nicely' dairy cows are treated – no matter if they're let out to graze in beautiful fields all year round – they all end up in the slaughterhouse. Their bodies and reproductive systems are exploited from the day they're born until the day they die – and when they stop producing enough milk to keep us happy their time is up.

All this, for a glass of milk or a piece of cheese.

Pigs

Among some of the most intelligent and emotionally complex animals in the world, pigs are more intelligent than dogs, who live as companion animals, and are proven to be as intelligent as a three-year-old human child. Almost all pigs are raised on intensive farms where their lives are grim from birth. Weak piglets are killed. If it's thought they won't survive until slaughter, they're deemed worthless, and undercover footage shows them being killed with iron bars or slammed against floors and walls. This official process is called 'thumping', or PAC – 'Pounding Against Concrete'. This form of death – by blunt trauma – is deemed 'humane'.

At just a couple of days old, piglets have their tails cut off and their teeth pulled, clipped or ground down. In many countries they're also castrated. All this is done without anaesthetic, and footage of these procedures shows piglets squealing in agony. Tail docking is rampant in the UK, USA, Europe and Australia. The industry insists it's necessary to stop pigs from harming each other – but the reason pigs become bored and aggressive is because they're forced to live in cramped conditions with no comfort or stimulation. This results in abnormal behaviour and stress. Giving pigs straw, wood and hay to root around in is helpful – but tail docking is quicker and cheaper. Pigs are so intelligent that UK law actually mandates they must have some form of mental stimulation in their environment. This is often just a hanging metal chain.

In the wild, pigs love to nest and forage. Female pigs have powerful maternal instincts, and they like to build cosy nests to give birth in. In most farms, sows are confined to farrowing crates for the last weeks of their pregnancy, and after they've given birth. There's no comfort here: made from concrete and metal, sows are unable to even turn around, causing extreme psychological distress. A sow wants to bond with her piglets but can't; trapped in her farrowing crate, she can't reach them. She can only lie on her side on the hard floor while they suckle from her. Some farmers point out that they throw in shredded paper so she can attempt to build a nest – but because sows can't even turn around, this action is utterly pointless.

At around three weeks, piglets are taken from their mothers to be fattened up. Because they haven't fed from their mothers long enough to build up immunity, they're pumped with antibiotics. In such cramped, filthy conditions, disease spreads quickly. An investigation by the Soil Association found that 63 per cent of pork tested contained antibiotic-resistant E. coli, the most common cause of urinary-tract infections and dangerous blood poisoning in humans, and a cause of meningitis.

After her piglets are taken, the sow is finally removed from her crate; now she will be impregnated again, and the cycle will repeat. When the sow is spent from the trauma – usually after four to seven pregnancies – she's sent to the slaughterhouse.

In the USA, there are more than 75 million pigs on factory farms on any given day[3], and around 120 million pigs killed each year. The average slaughterhouse kills about a thousand pigs an hour, meaning that any semblance of a 'humane', painless death is both illogical and improbable.

Over half of the nine million pigs slaughtered in the UK each year are killed in gas chambers. This is considered the most 'humane' mode of slaughter. Pigs are herded into metal cages that are lowered into pits full of carbon dioxide. Government reports have found that the gas causes serious welfare problems: pigs suffer from respiratory distress and hyperventilation, and footage from the chambers shows pigs squealing, panicking, climbing all over each other as they gasp for air. In traumatic footage taken by animal activists, the pigs' screams can be heard far outside the chambers. It can take thirty seconds for pigs to be rendered unconscious by the gas, and their screams continue all the while.

After the gas has rendered the pigs unconscious, they are shackled by their hind legs, hoisted in the air and then their throats are cut and they're drained of blood. Some of these pigs aren't yet unconscious from the gassing, and there are many reports from slaughterhouse workers stating that these pigs are still fully conscious and aware when they're dumped in a

_____

In the UK, the average chicken costs less than a pint of beer. This is the value we place on these animals' lives.

tank of boiling water. If they're still alive, this burns them and drowns them. A large metal paddle pushes them under water so they can't escape. They die while thrashing around in the scalding water.

Most pigs are ready to be killed from five months old. Sows are killed between three to five years. Pigs naturally live to twenty years old.

Sheep

The UK has one of the largest flocks in Europe, and around 14 million sheep are slaughtered every year. Globally, the vast majority of sheep are farmed extensively, meaning they're reared outdoors. Images of sheep grazing in picturesque fields lead many people to think that sheep farming is peaceful and happy – idyllic even, at least before the slaughter. But – and sorry for being such a constant source of bad news – that isn't the case.

Unlike cows, sheep are left outside all year, without any shelter. During freezing, snow-covered winters, there's no respite for sheep: they can't graze and they can't feed. With the rise in extreme weather, both flooding and the scorching sun can have fatal consequences for these defenceless animals. Around one in twenty sheep die of sickness, starvation or exposure.

Sheep naturally give birth to one lamb in the spring, but because farmers want to take advantage of the profitable spring lamb market and sell animals big enough to be eaten, many are choosing to lamb in winter. In the UK, this means that around four million lambs die in the harsh conditions – usually from cold, malnutrition or disease. Because it's more lucrative, ewes have been selectively bred to produce two or three lambs each pregnancy, and around 85 per cent of ewes now give birth to two or more lambs each year, causing strain on their bodies.

Shortly after they're born, lambs have their tails docked and males are castrated – painful mutilations that are often completely unnecessary. Both these mutilations can lead to serious injuries and sometimes death.

In spite of common opinion, sheep aren't stupid. A 2001 study found they recognized and remembered more than 50 different faces for longer than two years, and, like humans, they are drawn to smiles rather than frowns.[4] Other studies show that sheep learn to find their way out of complex mazes. They build meaningful friendships, grieve when their friends are taken to be slaughtered, and are one of the few species in the world that display lifelong preferences for the same sex (around eight per cent of rams are estimated to be gay).

In spite of their emotional intelligence and ability to feel pain, sheep suffer greatly during live export.

Millions of sheep are exported every year. In the UK, lambs as young as four weeks old are packed into overcrowded trucks and driven to destinations as far as Italy, Romania and Hungary. The journey itself is extremely uncomfortable and stressful, and EU law allows sheep to be transported for 14 hours without water or rest. This regulation is often broken and hardly ever enforced by authorities, so longer journey times are commonplace. Throughout the arduous journey, the amount of space each sheep has can be equal to three sheets of A4 paper.

On to wool now – something few people, unless they've looked into it, see a problem with. You're just giving the sheep a haircut, aren't you?

Sheep, naturally, don't need to be sheared. We've bred them to grow excess amounts of wool, and if cows have been turned into milk machines, then sheep can be considered wool machines. Shearers are usually paid by the amount of wool they shear, not by the hour, which means working as quickly as possible is most profitable. Rushing the shearing process leads to serious injury, and tails, teats and ears have all been documented as having been shorn off.

Countless investigations have revealed shocking cruelty at sheep farms, even on 'sustainable, ethical' farms. Shearers were shown punching, kicking and stamping on sheep, beating a lamb in the head with a hammer, twisting a sheep's neck until it was broken, hitting them in the face with electric clippers, and standing on their heads and necks. When animals are treated as commodities, abuse is simply par for the course.

And of course, sheep bred for their wool don't get to live out their lives frolicking on the hills. In Australia, three million sheep are exported as far as North Africa, on journeys that can last weeks. Whatever their destination, whatever their purpose, almost all sheep end up in the slaughterhouse.

Poultry

Poultry farming includes geese, turkeys, chickens and ducks, but more chickens are killed every year than all other land animals put together. Chicken used to be eaten rarely, as a treat: in 1950 the average Brit ate less than a single kilogram per year; now Britons eat around 25kg (55lb) each year – more than 2kg (4½lb) each month. In the UK, we eat more than two million chickens every day. In the USA, the number stands at around twenty-five million.

Just as there are two types of cattle farming – dairy and beef – so there are two types of chicken farming: chickens farmed for their meat ('broilers') and layer hens, which are farmed for their eggs.

Broiler chickens live short, miserable lives. While chickens can live naturally up to ten years, they're slaughtered at around six weeks old at intensive farms; free-range broilers are killed around eight weeks old. Intensive farms produce 94 per cent of the UK's chicken.[5]

Broiler chickens have been specially bred to get as big as possible, as quickly as possible. This rapid growth can cause all manner of health problems, and because their breasts are so oversized for their frame, often their legs can't support them. Undercover footage shot in 2019 shows that chickens reared by companies that supply three major supermarket chains were collapsing under their own weight.

The sheds broiler chickens live in are cleaned once every six weeks, after the chickens are taken to the slaughterhouse, and before the new, young chickens move in. The ammonia from the chicken faeces damages the birds' eyes and respiratory systems; they also develop ulcers and burns on their legs, chest and feet. They're fed copious amounts of antibiotics to keep them alive.

We have this image of chickens scratching around the farmyard, but this isn't a reality. Most chickens will never get to do what comes naturally to them. They never get to build a nest or have a dust bath. They will never feel the sun or breathe fresh air. In the UK, the average chicken costs less than a pint of beer. This is the value we place on these animals' lives.

Layer hens live longer – usually for one to two years. They exist for one purpose – laying eggs – and have been bred to produce an unnaturally large number of eggs. Because this depletes a hen's calcium level, it can result in brittle bones and fractures.

Battery cages – where the space hens have is the same size as an A4 sheet of paper – were outlawed in the EU in 2012, but they're still used throughout the world, particularly in the USA. In the place of battery cages, the UK now uses 'enriched cages' – basically, cages that are a tiny bit larger. To stop stressed

ANIMAL AGRICULTURE IS THE LEADING CAUSE OF SPECIES EXTINCTION, OCEAN DEAD ZONES, WATER POLLUTION AND HABITAT DESTRUCTION.

chickens pecking at each other in these confined conditions, even free-range hens have their beaks clipped at around a day old – a painful process that deprives them of their main sensory organ.

And what about all the newborn chicks? Males and females are separated on their first day of life. Males are worthless to the industry, so they're suffocated in plastic bags, ground up alive in high-speed grinders, or gassed. Whether you buy free-range or organic eggs, the culling of male chicks is standard procedure.

As with dairy cows, all layer hens will be sent to the slaughterhouse when they stop producing enough eggs. Whether raised for meat or eggs, all chickens meet the same end.

Fish and Sea Animals

For several reasons, fish aren't considered in the same way as land animals are. We can't interact with them in a meaningful way. They live in a different environment to us. Also – and I think this fact is very important – they can't make any sounds. It's easy to kid ourselves an animal isn't suffering when you can't hear its screams. No one would doubt, after watching slaughterhouse footage and hearing the horrific sounds dying land animals make, that they're in pain – but with fish, it's silent. It makes a big difference – and I say that from experience, as someone who carried on eating fish even after

I'd stopped eating other meat: I didn't think they suffered in the same way.

Fish are smart. Sometimes really smart. In spite of the widely held belief that fish have a three-second memory, studies have shown that fish are able to form lifelong memories. After reviewing nearly two hundred research papers and after years of studying fish behaviour, Australian biologist Culum Brown determined that 'in many areas such as memory, their cognitive powers match or exceed those of "higher" vertebrates, including non-human primates.' Fish can demonstrate 'Machiavellian intelligence', the ability to manipulate others by deception or reconciliation. They use tools – something we long believed only primates, octopuses and crows were capable of. They feel pain, and they suffer. But there are no welfare rules for fish. We don't even have official figures for how many are killed each year; the deaths are only recorded by weight. We know it's in the trillions.

Fish deaths are brutal. Hauled out of the ocean in huge nets, the change in pressure can cause their gills to collapse, their swim bladders to rupture and their eyes to pop out of their heads. They're often suffocated as they're crushed among the thrashing bodies of millions of their kind. Once they're unloaded onto the trawlers, they're often gutted alive. Footage of this happening shows them writhing in pain.

Fish farms are underwater battery farms: fish are contained within sunken cages, crammed in so tight they can't swim freely and are reduced to thrashing around in filthy water. To keep them alive in such disgusting conditions, they're dosed with drugs, and the runoff that's discharged into surrounding waters causes havoc with the environment.

And then there are crustaceans – including lobsters, crabs and shrimps – and cephalopods, which include octopuses and squid. Octopuses are so intelligent they were given honorary mammal rank in the Cambridge Declaration on Consciousness in 2012. They can navigate mazes and open childproof jars without instruction. Recently an octopus broke out of his tank at New Zealand's national aquarium in the middle of the night, travelled across the floor and escaped down a drainpipe into the sea. Yet in many countries they are eaten alive. While eating live octopuses used to be popular only in East Asia, several restaurants in the USA now serve live octopus to customers. In one video, people laugh as a small octopus tries to escape one diner's chopsticks.

Despite evidence showing they have a central nervous system and feel pain, lobsters and crabs are regularly boiled alive. These days, it's possible to order live lobsters online so you can kill them yourself. Sent from Canada, the lobster spends up to a week trapped in a container, suffering silently. The fact that you

can order and be sent a live animal to kill online
should be shocking – but we're so disconnected from
marine animals that this barely makes a ripple.

Can't We Just Treat Animals Really Well?

Now, I know that after reading this, some of you
will be thinking that it can't all be that bad. It's true
that some farms do have high standards of welfare.
It's true that there *are* small, local, organic farms
where the animals are let out to roam or to root,
where they're able to build nests and bond with their
young. But it's also true that in the grand scheme of
things, these farms are few and far between – and
many farms stealthily masquerade as high welfare
when we know they are not.

I have had a lot of conversations with people who
believe that if an animal is treated well, it's okay
to kill them. I've spoken to dozens of people who
have farmers in the family, or know friends who are
farmers, and swear blind that they love their animals
more than anything.

As much as I disagree with their ideology when it
comes to animals and their purpose, I'm not out to
demonize farmers. I know some farmers treat their
animals as well as they can, and want to ensure that
when the animal is eventually taken to be slaughtered,
it's as quick and painless as it can be. But this is
extremely uncommon.

The problem is that if your livelihood is based on profiting from selling an animal's body, or exploiting its body to sell the things that come out of it, you can never have its best interests at heart. No matter how fondly a farmer might feel for their animals, at the end of the day they're commodities. They're products. Farmers make money from killing and exploiting these animals – that's why they exist.

A man called Donald Watson founded The Vegan Society in 1944. He grew up on a Yorkshire farm in the 1920s, long before farming became as industrialized as it is today. What he saw made him realize that the gentle, pastoral image we have of farming was nothing more than an illusion. 'The idyllic scene was nothing more than death row,' he said, 'where every creature's days were numbered by the point at which it was no longer of service to human beings.'[6]

Is there any way this isn't true?

But this isn't about farms. It isn't about farmers. It isn't even about the industry. This is about the animals, millions of whom, right now, at this very moment, are being terrorized in gas chambers, or hoisted up by their legs to have their throats cut. No matter how well-treated animals are, their last moments will be ones of fear and pain.

There is no way to humanely kill an animal who doesn't want to be killed. There just isn't. There's no nice way to die. Death hurts and it's scary, whether you're a human or a cow or a pig.

Slaughterhouse footage isn't something most people want to watch, but I do think it's important to witness it at least once, even if it's just for a few minutes. Documentaries such as *Land of Hope and Glory* (2017) and *Dominion* (2018) are excellent, and they're available to watch for free online. While they're about farming in general, they do show some footage from slaughterhouses. Please watch them. Watch these animals fight with every inch of their lives to stay alive. See their fear, their confusion. See their sad, desperate attempts to escape.

And if you still eat animal products but can't bear to watch it, ask yourself why you're paying for it to happen? The animals live this – they experience every painful, brutal moment. The least we can do is bear witness.

A Moral Dilemma

Before we get back to the fun stuff, I want to address another point. The problem with animal agriculture today is not just that the scale of it is out of control – it's that it's totally unnecessary. There was a time when human beings needed to eat animals to survive, but that time is long gone. What we're doing to animals – and as a consequence, to our planet – is unnecessary and unavoidable.

Yes, there are cultures and countries where it's still necessary to eat animal products to survive. But we have a choice. We have supermarkets on our doorstep that offer all the nutrients and plant-based alternatives we need, and these products don't necessitate suffering and cruelty.

So while there are better ways to rear and kill animals than the way I've described here, why are we doing this at all if we don't need to?

There's no meaningful argument to carry on with this violent behaviour. People say it's the food chain, it's just natural order – but nothing about animal agriculture, where animals are artificially inseminated, selectively bred, mutilated, slaughtered and then packaged up in plastic, has anything to do with nature.

We'll unpick the different justifications for continuing to kill animals later, but before we conclude I want to say one final thing. Such is the scale of animal agriculture that one aspect is hard to grasp. We hear figures and stats about billions of animals being slaughtered each year. We know it's a lot, but our brains can't process how many animals this really is. It takes more than 31 years for a billion seconds to tick by. We kill more than a billion animals every six days. Every single hour, more than seven million land animals are killed. Every hour. And every single one of these seven million land animals is an individual. They're not products or commodities. They're living beings with a heart and a brain. They think and they feel – emotions including anxiety and fear and agony. Confusion, too. If you do still eat animal products, I want to ask you a favour. If you have a dog or cat near you right now – or any type of companion animal, whether it's a rabbit or a hamster or a chicken – please feel their breaths, the gentle rising of their chest. Feel the beating of their heart, which is keeping them alive. Stroke their head, which is full of feelings and memories. Do you doubt the animals you eat and exploit are just the same?

Animals are here with us – not for us. They have never done anything to us. The least we can do is return the favour.

Health

In spite of the ever-pervasive fear that eating a vegan diet will lead to an epidemic of protein and vitamin B12 deficiency, it turns out that removing all animal products from your diet can actually be very healthy. *Healthier*, dare I say.

The largest body of nutritional professionals in the USA, the Academy of Nutrition and Dietetics (AND), has said that vegan diets are: 'healthful, nutritionally adequate, and may provide health benefits for the prevention and treatment of certain diseases. These diets are appropriate for all stages of the life cycle, including pregnancy, lactation, infancy, childhood, adolescence, older adulthood, and for athletes. Vegetarians and vegans are at reduced risk of certain health conditions, including ischemic heart disease, type 2 diabetes, hypertension, certain types of cancer, and obesity.'[1]

That's the view from the top.

Personally, I've never felt healthier than I am today. When people make the switch to a properly planned plant-based diet, most report benefits such as having more energy, feeling lighter, sleeping better, their skin improving, having better functioning bowels. But the changes I noticed were more minimal – probably because I was already vegetarian. The one big difference I noticed, apart from improved skin, was to my sleeping patterns. I'd been an insomniac since my teens, but within weeks of going plant-based I was sleeping like a normal person. It was wonderful – and totally unexpected.

So what are the benefits according to science?

The Health Benefits of Veganism

One of the most far-reaching studies on the health benefits of plant-based diets was published in the *Journal of the American Heart Association* in 2019.[2] Unlike other studies, which examined groups with a narrow generalizability, this study followed the health of ten thousand adults over 29 years. It concluded that switching to a plant-based diet reduces the risk of dying from a heart attack or stroke by a third. But that's not all. The study also found that a plant-based diet can reduce the likelihood of dying early from *any* cause by a quarter.

Multiple studies show that a vegan diet can prevent, treat and even reverse some of the leading causes of death, such as heart disease, type 2 diabetes and high blood pressure. They also show that a plant-based diet doesn't only improve blood sugar levels, cholesterol levels and weight, but can also alleviate fatigue, anxiety and depression. In spite of many people fixating on the fact that plant-based diets are less rich in vitamin B12, when followed properly they almost always contain more antioxidants, fibre, potassium, magnesium and vitamins A, C and E.

We know that veganism is on the rise exponentially, but we might not be aware of how quickly it's rising among athletes – people whose health is their very livelihood. Elite athletes including tennis players Novak Djokovic, Serena and Venus Williams, and F1 champ Lewis Hamilton and heavyweight boxer David Haye, all follow plant-based diets, and have waxed lyrical about how much better they feel.

'My diet hasn't just changed my game, it's changed my life – my wellbeing,' Djokovic said. 'Eating vegan makes me more aware of my body on the court…more alert. I removed toxins from my body, and with them went all the inflammation and other things that were messing with my energy levels.' Djokovic has also cited his vegan diet as being one of the reasons why he recovers so well – and a faster recovery time is an oft-cited perk of a plant-based diet.

'I don't have the soreness I used to have before,' American footballer David Carter said of the unexpected benefits of switching to a plant-based diet. 'I'm not sluggish. I recover a lot faster. I have more energy. I'm a lot stronger than I was before.' And, at 1.96m (6ft 5in) and around 136kg (300lb), it's also worth mentioning that he's definitely getting enough protein. So why are people convinced veganism isn't healthy?

Before we dig deeper into the science behind the ways consuming animal products can cause disease, it's important to examine why the belief that we need to eat them to be healthy is so widely held – and why, in spite of the evidence, many people refuse to believe the facts.

Manipulation and Myths

Since we were young, most of us have been fed myths by the meat, dairy and egg industries. We were told that drinking milk builds strong bones, that eggs are the best way to start your day, that eating meat makes you strong. We know the meat, dairy and egg industries spend vast amounts of money concealing the truth of animal agriculture via marketing and advertising, labelling and packaging – and they apply this same tactic in terms of health. Animals aren't the only ones being harmed by the deception of big business; we are, too.

In the USA, the Department of Agriculture spends hundreds of billions of dollars each year on advertising government-backed sales of meat, dairy products and eggs. The money and power these types of companies have is, frankly, frightening. Let's look at some examples.

DAIRY

Dairy products are among the top sources of saturated fat, a major contributor to heart disease, type 2 diabetes and Alzheimer's disease. Studies also link dairy consumption to a higher risk of breast, ovarian and prostate cancers. But so many of us believe milk is healthy – necessary, even.

One of the most pervasive myths is that milk builds strong bones – but a comprehensive Harvard study followed 72,000 women for twenty years and found zero evidence that milk prevents either bone fractures or osteoporosis.[3] Another study of more than 96,000 people found that the more milk men drank as adolescents, the more bone fractures they experienced in later life.[4] This is because dairy products are acid-forming foods, which means that without counterbalancing alkalizing foods, they can promote a pH imbalance in the body that causes calcium to be stripped from the bones.

Cow's milk is, obviously, breast milk for baby cows. It's absolutely healthy – if you're a 22kg (50lb) calf hoping to grow into a 450kg (1,000lb) cow. The only breast milk humans need is the milk from our own mothers – and not past the age of about two. But don't just take my word for it. 'Humans have no nutritional requirement for animal milk, an evolutionarily recent addition to the diet,' says Dr Walter Willett, Professor of Medicine at Harvard Medical School.[5]

But once again, people are being deceived by the dairy industry, their health gambled with for a quick buck. With more and more evidence coming out that dairy, actually, doesn't give you strong bones and isn't in any way necessary in the human diet, the industry started to fight back. In 2017, a study was published stating that children who drank plant-based milk instead of cow's milk were shorter than their peers. The unspoken implication was that their poor, deficient, plant-based bones just couldn't grow as quickly. So what's the problem with this study?

The problem was that the lead author was Jonathon L Maguire, who has a troubling history of receiving funding from the dairy industry. Maguire admitted to receiving $10,000 from the dairy industry[6], but actually he received $90,000 from the Dairy Farmers of Canada[7], and an undisclosed amount from the Dairy Farmers of Ontario.[8] Despite his denials about being involved with dairy industry advisory committees, in 2016 he sat on the board of the Dairy Farmers of Canada Expert Scientific Advisory Committee.[9]

In 2014, another study published by Maguire found that cow's milk is vital for obtaining vitamin D – yet failed to mention that vitamin D isn't even naturally found in milk: it's fortified with it. So the study could have just as accurately said 'Vitamin D supplements are vital for obtaining vitamin D.'

Maguire's assertion that cow's milk is necessary for optimal growth rests on the fact that it contains protein and fat – nutrients that are abundantly available in countless other sources, ones that don't contain high levels of cholesterol and saturated fat. When asked whether children could meet their nutritional needs without consuming cow's milk, Maguire inexplicably replied, 'I don't actually know the answer to that question.'[10] Okay, doctor.

This type of furtive alliance is rampant, and it's just the same in the UK. In 2017, the Royal Osteoporosis Society warned that dairy-free diets could be a 'ticking time bomb' for young people's bone health. Their report was broadcast over dozens of news sites including the BBC. But no one mentioned that the Royal Osteoporosis Society receives funds from – you guessed it! – a dairy company.[11]

In 2017, British newspaper the *Guardian* reported a study at Reading University, which found that cheese doesn't raise the risk of heart attack or stroke after all.[12] This 'international team of experts' wanted to challenge the belief that cheese and dairy is bad for you. 'While it is a widely held belief,' Reading University professor Ian Gives said, 'our research shows that that's wrong.' A closer look at the study shows a note regarding 'conflict of interest'. Can you guess what it is? The study was part-funded by the three pro-dairy groups Global Dairy Platform, Dairy Research Institute and Dairy Australia.[13]

We should be outraged. These claims are not only untrue, but also nefarious because of the harm they cause people.

Why are people insisting that we need to drink milk from a cow when there are so many other healthier alternatives? Plant-based milks contain all the same nutritional benefits as cow's milk, without any of the negatives. They're rich in vitamins, minerals and fibre, have a good combination of mono- and polyunsaturated fats, and are easily digested. Most of them are low in fat, and none of them contains cholesterol. Almost all are fortified with calcium, vitamin B12 and, like dairy, vitamin D. Soya milk contains the same amount of protein as cow's milk, but because dairy proteins such as whey and casein are hard to digest, it's better protein too.

In the USA, the Physicians' Committee for Responsible Medicine – a non-profit organization with 12,000 doctor members – is urging the government to be open about the harm dairy can do. In a statement, it didn't mince words: 'You have stomach cramps, pain, bloating? Stop eating dairy. You have arthritis? Stop eating dairy. You want to lose weight? Stop eating dairy. You have or are at risk for heart disease and need to avoid saturated fat? Stop eating dairy, the number-one source of saturated fat in the American diet. You are at risk for prostate, ovarian, and breast cancer? Stop eating dairy.'[14]

EGGS

Since 1956, people in the UK have been told that starting your day with eggs is the best way. The Egg Marketing Board used the advertising slogan 'Go to work on an egg' through the 1950s and 1960s, and it stuck pretty well. The ad made no health or nutritional claims – it just told us to go to work on an egg. And many of us did.

Across the pond, the American Egg Board were also thinking about how to market their eggs, but they wanted to make some health claims. While individual egg companies can say pretty much whatever they want, if you want the American Egg

Board to fund your adverts, you're not allowed to lie. This is because the board is appointed by the federal government. In 2015, emails between egg companies looking to promote their product and the Department of Agriculture were revealed, and what they exposed about the way in which such companies and governments work together is fascinating.[15]

One egg company wanted to promote eggs in a brochure about kids' healthy snacks. But because of laws against false advertising, the Department of Agriculture rejected this suggestion. 'The words nutritious and healthy carry certain connotations, and because eggs have the amount of cholesterol they do, plus the fact that they're not low in fat, [the words healthy and nutritious] are problematic.'

Then the Department of Agriculture kindly offered some advice. While saying that eggs were 'nutritious and healthy' was untrue and therefore against the law, the egg company *could* say they were 'nutrient-dense'. Why? Because 'nutrient-dense' has no legal definition: triple-fried chips can be called nutrient-dense. Vodka can be called nutrient-dense.

Then, in another ad campaign, the egg industry wanted to refer to eggs as 'nutritional powerhouses that aid in weight loss.' The Department of Agriculture blocked that too, reminding the egg company that because of the fat and cholesterol content, eggs can't be portrayed as a diet food. They also can't be called 'nutritional powerhouses'. The egg company kept at it: what about 'Egg-ceptional Nutrition'? No, that wasn't allowed either – you can't imply eggs are nutritious, remember?

So in the end, the slogan was 'Find true satisfaction' – and because the company couldn't say eggs aided weight loss, they plumped for 'can reduce hunger'. Eating food reduces hunger! A wily campaign indeed. Then the egg company and the Department of Agriculture all gave themselves a pat on the back.

But these exchanges are important, because not only do they show the buddying up between the industries and the authorities, but they also highlight just how harmful eggs can be. These industry memos also revealed that eggs, by law, can't even be referred to as 'safe' or 'safe to eat' due to the prevalence of salmonella poisoning. Legally, eggs can't even be called a 'rich source of protein' because – according to the Department of Agriculture – they aren't.

The bottom line is that eggs are extremely high in cholesterol. The average egg contains about 200mg of cholesterol – that's almost three times the amount in a Big Mac. A single egg has more cholesterol than your body requires – and actually, because our bodies naturally produce more cholesterol than the amount we need, any added cholesterol that comes from food is unnecessary. A plant-based diet is the only diet that's cholesterol free.

Around sixty per cent of an egg's calories come from fat, and much of that's saturated. Saturated fat and cholesterol lead to heart disease, type 2 diabetes and certain types of cancer. A meta-analysis of 14 studies found that eggs conclusively increase the risk of heart disease and diabetes.[16] Research showed that participants who consumed the most eggs had up to a 68 per cent increased chance of developing heart disease and diabetes when compared to the participants who ate the fewest eggs. For participants who already had diabetes, the chance of developing heart disease from eating eggs jumped by 83 per cent.

We all want a protein-packed, filling start to the day, but promoting the idea that eggs are the way to achieve this is irresponsible. I once wondered what I'd eat in the mornings if I cut out eggs, but now my breakfasts are healthier, tastier and more diverse than ever. I have overnight oats with peanut butter and berries, breakfast burritos, coconut yogurt with fruit and chia, scrambled tofu on toast, superfood smoothies or smoothie bowls, veggie sausages and beans, chickpeas and avocado on toast, three-ingredient pancakes made from bananas, oats and plant-based milk. If you're in a rush, you can't beat some pitta and hummus: high in protein, iron, folate, fibre, phosphorus and B vitamins, it's also totally delicious.

MEAT

People who buy meat generally want to know it hasn't been tampered with too much. Most people don't *want* their meat to come packed with preservatives or hormones or whatever else goes into certain types of meat products. But when it comes to determining what 'natural' meat is, the US Department of Agriculture plays fast and loose with the term: to them, 'natural' just means that the meat has been minimally processed and has no artificial ingredients. Antibiotics, hormones and preservatives can be pumped into the meat in abundance.[7]

In 2015, the expert panel who were advising the government on the Dietary Guidelines for Americans had a sensible suggestion. They wanted to include information advising people to eat less meat. According to 'consistent evidence', the Dietary Guidelines Advisory Committee said, 'a dietary pattern that is higher in plant-based foods...and lower in animal-based foods is more health promoting and is associated with lesser environmental impact.'[8]

The meat industry weren't having it. They disputed the claims and refuted the evidence – and they won. 'Moving forward, we hope the agencies will continue to focus on the clear science highlighting the wide variety of nutrition benefits of all meat and poultry products,' said Barry Carpenter, the President of the North American Meat Institute.[19] What could be Barry's incentive for this clear refusal of science?

The World Health Organization has clearly stated that processed meat is a major contributor to cancer, declaring it 'carcinogenic to humans'.[20] Studies show that just a small amount of processed meat – one sausage or a couple of strips of bacon – significantly increases the risk of prostate cancer, breast cancer, pancreatic cancer, colorectal cancer, as well as overall cancer mortality. A National Institutes of Health study of more than half a million people also found that eating processed meat increased the risk of heart disease, the world's biggest killer.[21]

But it isn't just processed meat. Red meat increases the risk of kidney failure, according to a study of more than 63,000 participants.[22] People who ate the most protein from red meat increased their chances of kidney failure, while replacing servings of red meat with other proteins such as soya products or legumes cut the risk by more than sixty per cent.

Another very recent study (September 2019) in the *American Journal of Clinical Nutrition* found that red and white meat raise cholesterol levels equally.[23] The researchers concluded that their findings supported eating meatless protein sources, and that white meat was the same as red meat when it comes to heart disease risk.

By taking the advice of these experts and advising the public to eat more plant-based foods, the US government had a unique chance to protect not just the environment, but also the health of their people. They didn't take it.

The abundance of plant-based mock meats around today is staggering. Every supermarket sells them. Whether it's made from tofu or tempeh or jackfruit, whether it's soya protein or pea protein or seitan, vegan 'meat' is having a revolution. The unprecedented success of Beyond Meat and Impossible Foods proves that our interest in, and appetite for, plant meat isn't going anywhere. When compared to a typical beef burger, the Beyond Meat patty contains more protein and iron, but less fat and zero cholesterol. It also uses 99 per cent less water and 93 per cent less land, emits 90 per cent fewer greenhouse gases and uses 46 per cent less energy. And of course, it didn't necessitate the suffering and death of a gentle, sentient animal.

At this point, it's just the logical choice.

FISH

Okay, so we know fish is healthy. Everyone knows fish is healthy. Right? Well...

We've already looked at the dairy industry's favourite myth – the idea that we need to drink milk for strong bones. But the fish industry has one that's worked even better: 'fish for omega-3!' Now it is true that some fish contains high levels of omega-3 fatty acids. But it's also true that fish isn't the only source of omega-3 fatty acids. In Chapter 3 we'll look at the best sources of plant-based omega-3s, but what it's important to note here is that plant-based sources of omega-3 contain absolutely nothing unhealthy. Nothing in them can harm you. Not so for fish.

One reason many people eat fish is for their essential fatty acids, because they want to protect their heart. But 15–30 per cent of the fat in fish is saturated, which means our livers produce more cholesterol, which clogs up our arteries. This will not protect our hearts. People have this blanket assumption that seafood is healthy, yet few people are aware of the high cholesterol levels in many species: 150g (6oz) of shrimp contains 322mg of cholesterol. A Big Mac contains 75mg.

Earlier we looked briefly at the pollution in our waters (see page 37). Our rivers and oceans are contaminated with runoff from animal agriculture, raw sewage, toxic chemicals, microplastics and general waste. Because fish live in these same waters, mercury builds up in their bodies, and many of the fish with the highest concentrations of mercury are the ones people eat most: halibut, tuna, Chilean sea bass, blue crab, king mackerel, marlin, swordfish, sturgeon, grouper, snapper and so on.

Mercury poisoning can lead to nervous system disorders, reproductive problems and developmental issues in children and unborn foetuses. A study by the Environmental Working Group found that people who ate the advised amounts of many frequently eaten fish were consuming high levels of mercury – while getting little omega-3 benefit.[24]

Many of us have this idea that fish is fresh and healthy, but let's bear in mind the reality of farmed fish – which counts for more than half of all fish eaten.[25] Because fish farms are so cramped, with thousands of fish thrashing around in small pens, the water soon becomes filthy, and disease and parasites quickly spread. To counteract this, antibiotics and pesticides are added to the water, which the fish eat and absorb – and we in turn eat and absorb when we eat the fish.

The Science

We know that the meat, dairy and egg industries have influenced scientific research, advertising and even government information, to make us think we need to eat animal products to be healthy. We also know that consuming animal products can lead to an increased risk of several diseases. Let's examine the evidence by looking at some studies – ones that haven't been funded by the dairy industry.

HEART DISEASE

The biggest killer in the world is heart disease.
In the USA, 610,000 people die every year from
it[26] – that's one in four deaths. In the UK, the
stats are similar: around 170,000 heart-disease-
related deaths are recorded each year[27], more
than a quarter of all deaths. Other factors play a
part – smoking, drinking, stress – but extremely
common risk factors, according to the British
Heart Foundation, are high cholesterol, high blood
pressure, type 2 diabetes and obesity. All of these
factors are exacerbated by eating animal products,
which are high in both low-density lipoprotein
(LDL) cholesterol, known as 'bad' cholesterol, and
saturated fat.

LDL cholesterol is only found in animal protein,
and because of this, a vegan diet is the only diet
that's entirely free of it. Animal products such as
fatty meat, processed meat, milk, cheese and butter
also contain high levels of saturated fat, which
actually affects our LDL levels more than eating
cholesterol. This is because saturated fat causes
our livers to make even more cholesterol, and this
cholesterol forms artery-blocking plaques which
increase the chances of heart attack or stroke.

In 2017, a comprehensive review of 49 studies
by researchers from the Physicians' Committee for
Responsible Medicine in the USA found that plant-

based diets lower cholesterol levels more effectively than any other diet.[28] When compared to omnivorous diets, plant-based diets typically reduce LDL levels by up to thirty per cent.[29]

Obesity is another factor that increases a person's risk of heart disease. In the USA, nearly forty per cent[30] of the population are obese. In the UK[31] and Australia[32], it's 28 per cent. Aside from heart disease, obesity can lead to other life-threatening conditions such as type 2 diabetes, certain types of cancer, including breast cancer and bowel cancer, and stroke. Multiple studies show that vegetarians are generally slimmer than people who eat meat, but vegans have the lowest body mass index of all.[33]

High blood pressure, or hypertension, is another contributing factor to heart disease. Studies have repeatedly found that vegans have the lowest rates of hypertension.[34]

A wholefood plant-based diet is the only diet that's been shown to prevent, treat and reverse heart disease. If we know that veganism can treat and even prevent the world's biggest killer, shouldn't our governments be trying to promote it, not quash it?

TYPE 2 DIABETES

According to the International Diabetes Federation, around 642 million people will be living with diabetes by 2040. In the UK, around 4.5 million people are already diagnosed with it; in the USA, the number stands at more than thirty million. The most common type of diabetes is type 2 – this counts for ninety per cent of all diabetes cases. Unlike type 1 diabetes, which is believed to be caused by genes and environmental factors, type 2 is largely caused by a person's way of life.

Nearly 15 per cent of all global deaths are attributed to diabetes, and it's also frequently linked to depression, which in turn affects how well blood glucose levels are regulated. A systematic review of the available evidence was published in the *British Medical Journal* in 2018. The research found that a predominantly vegan diet seems to be best for keeping type 2 diabetes in check[35] because plant-based diets are generally lower in saturated fat and higher

---

If we know that veganism can treat and even prevent the world's biggest killer, shouldn't our governments be trying to promote it, not quash it?

in fibre, fruit, vegetables and other health-boosting substances such as phytochemicals and antioxidants.

Based on their studies, researchers concluded that vegan diets can 'significantly improve psychological health, quality of life, HbA1c [blood sugar] levels and weight, and therefore the management of diabetes.'

Final Reflections

The good news is that as veganism rises in popularity, people are becoming more curious about plant-based diets. People who eat meat are often happy to try vegan dishes and products, and though many still doubt the health benefits of plant based diet, awareness of the dangers of meat and dairy is at an all-time high.

Plant milk sales are surging at unprecedented rates. People are waking up to the enormous harm dairy causes – not just to our own health, but also to our planet and, of course, to cows. In 2018 dairy milk sales in the USA dropped by $1.1 billion. In the UK, almost a quarter of us now drink plant milk. The dairy industry is crumbling, and knowing what we now do, it's a beautiful thing to behold.

There are some who look at the declining sales of animal products and say it's just a fleeting fad. That it's transient – like veganism itself. What these people fail to understand is that it's all part of a permanent

MY DIET HASN'T JUST CHANGED MY GAME, IT'S CHANGED MY LIFE – MY WELLBEING

Novak Djokovic

change. This is part of our imminent and irreversible evolution towards a kinder, more just, more evolved world. The recognition that we're destroying our planet for the sake of a burger cannot be undone. The understanding that animals are sentient beings who have feelings and purpose cannot be reversed. Because of this, all attempts to downplay the dietary changes we're making, all efforts to diminish veganism as a passing fad, are doomed to fail.

Now I know there will be some people who still can't bear the idea of saying a final farewell to their favourite animal products, whether it's the occasional steak or some slices of cheese. A question I hear a lot – and one I once wondered myself – often comes up: 'Can't I just eat animal products in moderation?'

Yes, of course you can. It's true that if you eat only very small amounts of meat, dairy, eggs or fish, you can very probably avoid causing serious harm to your health. But it's also true that even the smallest amount of meat, dairy, eggs or fish still causes harm. Because, really, this isn't just about our personal health – it's about the full picture. The environmental destruction, the silent suffering, billions of brutal deaths. Each time we buy a box of eggs or a wedge of cheese or a pack of bacon, we're sending a message to these destructive industries that we want them to continue. It's a vote for oppression. Choosing a plant-based alternative is a vote for progression.

Doing it less is better than doing it more, of course. But it's interesting that veganism is the only social justice movement where we talk about *minimizing* the harm. When we recognize that a certain behaviour is harmful, we understand we need to eradicate it. We don't have 'Racist Wednesdays' or 'Sexist Saturdays'. We talk about ending the behaviour altogether. So eating less meat, fish, dairy and eggs is better than eating more, or even eating the same. But it's not as good as not eating any.

So rather than asking the question 'Can't I just eat animal products in moderation?', let's ask some new questions.

If you knew you didn't need to eat animals' bodies, or the things that come out of them, to be healthy... If you knew you could not only survive but thrive on a plant-based diet...If you knew going vegan is the only way you could never intentionally hurt animals...If you knew that eating this way was infinitely better for our environment and the future of our planet...Would you still choose to kill animals?

STARTING
OUT

Okay, so you think you want to go vegan? Great! Or maybe you think you want to start moving towards a kinder, more sustainable way of living without putting too much pressure on yourself. Well, that's still great! There aren't set rules to going vegan. Sure, once you're vegan you don't eat or buy animal products, but in terms of actually getting there, there isn't one single roadmap.

I know one person who watched the documentary *Cowspiracy* (2014) and went from eating meat to full vegan, overnight. I know other people who slowly transitioned towards a plant-based lifestyle by way of omission: first they went veggie, then they cut out dairy, then they cut out eggs. Alternatively, you could start by having one or two days in the week when you only eat plant-based food, and gradually add on an extra vegan day until you're eating plant-based food all week.

So which approach is right for you? Go with your gut. If you have that lightbulb moment when you make the connection and can't bear the thought of eating animals – or the things that come out of them – then why not try to make the full switch at once?

It's absolutely doable. There are a few things you need to know first (and we'll get to them very soon!).

But if you feel totally overwhelmed at the thought of cutting out all animal products at once, there's nothing wrong with transitioning towards being fully plant-based over a period of time. It's true that in terms of our environment and the fate of billions of animals, we don't have the luxury of time – but it's also true that veganism is a journey, and everyone has a different way, and time, of getting there.

Going vegan is not a sacrifice or a chore. It is a joy, a journey that should excite and inspire you – not make you feel daunted or hesitant. Move forward at your own pace, try new things, experiment. And feel positive about it all: you're doing something powerful.

One thing that's important to know when you're starting out is that it doesn't take long for your mindset to change. Your brain evolves as you do, and you just don't look at certain foods the way you used to. The thought that I would ever be repulsed by cheese would have once been impossible to fathom, but after a few months of being vegan I walked past a cheese shop, caught a whiff of sour milk and was almost sick. When I see slices of cheese now, I can't help but see the cruelty and death that comes with it. So give yourself time. Allow your thought processes to evolve.

Always remember that veganism is not a pursuit for perfection. It's about trying to do the least harm and the most good. It's also a learning curve, an organic progression, and if you start off with flexible guidelines you may find yourself naturally becoming more vigilant as time passes.

Because it's not about being perfect, if you happen to 'fall off the wagon' and eat something non-vegan, it's not the end of the world. Pick yourself up and hop back on. Never let anyone belittle you or try to shame you. There will, unfortunately, always be that person who'll try to poke holes in your armour – who'll see you eating crisps containing milk powder and come striding towards you, eyes gleaming, and say 'Aha! Not so vegan after all!' Screw those people. Seriously. If demeaning someone who's trying to reduce the harm they cause is what gets them off, then allow them that small joy. You've got more important things to do.

If you want, you could always tell people you're 'trying' to be vegan. That way, you've given yourself leeway until you feel confident enough to own your decision and say, 'Yes, I'm vegan!' Because for a lot of people, that's scary. I know a lot of vegans who prefer to describe their diets as 'plant based', just because they feel it's less 'controversial' and is less likely to illicit weird responses from people. No matter how much you might agree with the principles behind veganism, calling yourself 'vegan' and committing publicly to this lifestyle can be daunting. I know it was for me at one stage – and I was already veggie! I didn't want to be thought of as 'a vegan'. There was a stigma around it, I felt. I didn't want people to think I was boring, or obsessed with kale or quinoa, or that I hugged trees and only wore hemp. Luckily, though, the astonishing rise of veganism means these tired tropes are fast becoming obsolete.

Personally, I refer to myself as 'vegan' rather than 'plant based' because I want to normalize the word. You don't have to be a lentil-swilling health-freak hippie to be vegan. You just have to care about something – about animals, about the planet, about your own health. And really, as long as you're trying to eat in a way that's kinder, who the hell cares what you call it?

The single best piece of advice I can give is to make sure you're supported. Signing up to a free vegan organization that will support and guide you through the transition will be the most useful thing you can do (see Chapter 6 for more information and tips on support).

You also become part of a community, which is another important factor in making the change easier. If you're the only person on this journey, it can sometimes seem lonely and daunting; there's no one to sound off on, or share your experiences with. The vegan community – aka the V-gang – is huge, diverse, warm and welcoming. We *love* helping would-be vegans, or answering questions from people who are just curious about this lifestyle and want to know more. If you're active on social media, follow plant-based chefs, vloggers, doctors, fitness gurus and educators. Not only will this give your knowledge a serious boost, but it's inspiring. For me, it was seeing super-ripped plant-based athletes showcasing their workout routines, and vegan vloggers on YouTube sharing their incredible-looking food that got me raring to go.

Staying Healthy

When people first go plant based, or cut a large portion of animal products from their diet, they often report experiencing similar effects: their skin is brighter, they have more energy, they generally feel 'lighter'. Weight loss is often an unintended outcome. All that fibre means your trips to the toilet will likely become a lot more regular. Well, better out than in! But remember, this usually only occurs while your body is getting used to these changes; after a month or so you'll settle right down – although being as regular as clockwork is another healthy perk of being plant based. Honestly, even going to the toilet is more fun when you're vegan.

To reap all the benefits of a vegan lifestyle, it's vital to start the change in a proactive, informed manner. If you don't prepare adequately you might wake up on day one of trying to be vegan and find you have an empty kitchen – or a kitchen filled with products you can't eat. This isn't the best way to start. If you're used to getting key nutrients from animal products, you need to figure out which plant-based foods contain them, to keep you healthy and ward off fatigue. The last thing you want is for people to see you yawning and assume that a plant-based diet is bringing you down. Not so!

In this section we'll be covering the key nutrients you need and which foods contain them. But first, let's consider a few questions that new vegans or prospective vegans often have.

Is a Vegan Diet Healthy?

The answer to this is yes – if you're eating a healthy vegan diet. The idea that all plant-based food is healthy is sadly not true, and vegan burgers, cakes and shakes aren't necessarily going to be healthy just because they're vegan (sorry!). The good news is that plant-based food contains no cholesterol, which is only found in animal protein – but the bad news is that plant-based food can still contain saturated fat, high amounts of sugar and salt, artificial flavourings and so on.

There are, essentially, two very different types of vegan diet – and subsequently, two very different types of vegan. First, there are wholefood plant-based diets. These are based on foods such as fruits, vegetables, wholegrains, legumes, nuts and seeds – basically, all the things you *should* be eating; the stuff that's good for you. This type of diet tends to avoid refined ingredients, such as sugar, processed oils, white flour and so on, as much as possible.

Then, there's plant-based junk food – the stuff you buy packed up in supermarkets: vegan pizza, burgers, sausages, cheeses. Anything that's pretending to be something else (for example, vegan bacon, vegan hotdogs) is almost always processed, and therefore can't be considered a wholefood.

When people think you need to eat meat to be as strong as an ox, they're missing the most important fact: the ox eats grass.

That's not to say that all mock-meat foods are unhealthy, however. Products that are made from tofu or seitan (a plant-based 'meat' made from wheat gluten) can be great sources of protein – but some of these products contain a ton of fats, oils and E numbers. Similarly, vegan pizza can be pretty healthy if it has a thin base (preferably wholegrain) and is piled high with veggies – but if it's loaded with super-salty tomato sauce and a ton of plant-based cheese (usually very high in fat – just like dairy cheese) then it's not so healthy.

When I first started out, I was a proud junk food vegan. I was eager to show people that vegan food wasn't all couscous or salad leaves, but could be quick and indulgent too. A lot of people don't want to think they'll never be able to enjoy creamy pasta any more, or never be able to bite into a succulent burger that drips juice down your wrist. I wanted to show people that you can eat dirty on a vegan diet. Greasy chips, loaded nachos, sugar-laden cakes…Yep, you can have all that while eating a plant-based diet. Yay! But obviously, common sense, science and your own body would urge you to eat a predominantly wholefood plant-based diet.

It's worth mentioning here that going vegan often changes the way you think about lots of issues. I went vegan solely because of the animal factor, but the more I read, the more invested I became in environmental issues. Similarly, the more I discovered about the health benefits of a plant-based lifestyle, the more conscious I became about what I was putting into my body, and whether or not I was getting the right nutrients. (This is one of the many awesome things about going vegan: it makes you grow and evolve as a person.)

Now I follow the 80/20 rule: 80 per cent of the time I eat healthy, fresh wholefoods, and the other 20 per cent I'm more relaxed. That may mean having one day a week where I eat (and drink) whatever I want, or adding some plant-based chicken and cheese to my otherwise healthy, wholefoods dinner.

Be healthy and kind to your body, but treat yourself, if you want. Don't get obsessed. Life is about balance.

Can I Really Get All the Nutrients I Need on a Vegan Diet?

The short answer is yes. One thousand times yes.

When you go vegan – or tell people you're trying to go vegan – you'll likely discover that many people close to you are actually secretly trained in nutrition and they're all very concerned about your health. Be prepared to answer a whole bunch of questions like: 'How are you going to get enough calcium if you're not drinking milk?', 'Aren't vegans always vitamin B12 deficient?', 'Won't you become anaemic without animal products?' And the most prevalent question of all: 'But where do you get your protein from?' (Fun fact: that question is so rife in the world of veganism that it was almost the title for this book.)

Here's what you need to know about your key nutrients.

PROTEIN

Let's start with the biggie: protein. There's a reason hospital wings aren't packed full of feeble, protein-deficient vegans lamenting their plant-based diets. That reason is: almost all food contains protein. There's protein in potatoes, pasta, bread, fruits, vegetables. If you're getting enough calories and eating a balanced diet, you'll get enough protein by default. *Really*! You couldn't become protein deficient if you tried. Plant-based wholefoods that are especially high in protein include beans and lentils, beansprouts, tofu, wholegrains, nuts, seeds, hummus – to name just a few.

If you're not super-healthy, there's still no need to worry. Peanut butter and plant milks are high in protein, and many of the plant-based 'meats' that exist, such as soya and seitan, contain more protein than real meat. For example, 100g (3½oz) of 'Tofurky' sausages contain 29g (just under 1oz) of protein, while

100g (3½oz) of pork sausages contain around 17g (just over ½oz) of protein.

People tend to grossly overstate the amount of protein they need. Most people need only 50–60g (around 2oz) of protein a day, and you can easily get this from a healthy, balanced, plant-based diet. It's true that athletes and people who exercise a lot do need more protein – and we'll address that very soon.

As we've already seen, many elite athletes follow plant-based diets (see page 79). Other world-class vegan athletes include Kendrik Farris (Olympic weightlifter), Bryant Jennings (professional boxer), Nimai Delgado (pro bodybuilder) and Patrik Baboumian (world record-holding strongman). Have a quick Google: does anyone really think they're not getting enough protein?

When Lewis Hamilton decided to bulk up and gained 6.8kg (15lb), he spoke out about the misconceptions surrounding plant-based diets: 'Adding weight was easy and I did this on a vegan diet. People say, "Oh I need my protein and that's why I could never go vegan." I have plenty of protein in my diet and I've gained muscle.'

The main point to remember here is that almost everything we eat contains protein. When people think you need to eat meat to be as strong as an ox, they're missing the most important fact: the ox eats grass.

CALCIUM

The idea that cows' milk builds strong bones is one of the biggest dietary myths around. As we saw in Chapter 2, the dairy industry spends vast sums of money to spread the message that humans somehow need to drink the milk of a large bovine animal to stay healthy. That's why this particular myth, which is so strange when you actually think about it, is so pervasive.

It's helpful to know some facts here, so when well-meaning people enquire about your calcium levels, you can address their concerns. The fact is, there is no real scientific proof whatsoever backing up the idea that cows' milk makes human bones strong (see page 81). Studies stating otherwise are almost always funded by the dairy industry.

But we do, of course, need calcium in our diets – and luckily we can find plenty of it in plant-based foods. Green leafy vegetables such as kale, collard greens and watercress are high in calcium, as is broccoli, sweet potato, butternut squash and swede. Tahini and sesame seeds are also high in calcium – and, as an added bonus, contain more protein than milk and most nuts. White beans, almonds, figs, and poppy and chia seeds are calcium dense, as are edamame beans and tofu.

Happily, most plant milks are fortified with calcium, so you really don't have to try hard to get your calcium quota, even if you're not planning on being a 'wholefood vegan'.

VITAMIN B12

The vitamin that vegans probably need to take the most care not to become deficient in is B12. B12 is produced by bacteria that live in the soil and in the guts of animals (including humans), and this super-important vitamin is essential for cell production and nerve formation. The good news is that countless products are now fortified with B12 – from plant milks to breakfast cereals, to plant-based cheeses and mock meats. Just check the label. Marmite is also fortified with B12, as are most brands of nutritional yeast (an essential ingredient for any vegan kitchen, which we'll look at soon).

If you're worried you won't get enough B12 – or the people around you are worried – just take a supplement. And if you think that's unnatural, consider this: B12 is found in soil, which means that animals who are factory farmed are deficient in B12 as they don't even get to touch soil, let alone consume it when they eat grass. To counteract this deficiency, animals are fed B12 supplements – in fact, ninety per cent of all B12 supplements are fed to farmed animals.[1] Considering that the vast majority of meat is factory farmed, this means that, either way, most people are already getting their

B12 from supplements. You can either take it in the form of a pill yourself, or filter that supplement through another being's dead body. Your call.

IRON

The last thing you want as a vegan is to become anaemic. It'll be unpleasant for you, and it'll also give certain people the chance to say, 'See, vegans are always deficient!'

Anaemia is by no means a vegan issue – it's pretty common across the board, especially in women – and just like with protein, if you're eating a balanced diet there should be no reason why you're not getting enough iron. Once again, green leafy vegetables are your friend – kale, cabbage, watercress – as are vegan favourites tofu, beans, lentils and oats. Try snacking on dried fruits such as apricots, dates and figs – all high in iron – as well as Brazil nuts, almonds, pumpkin seeds and sesame seeds.

OMEGA-3

Along with its buddy omega-6, omega-3 is an essential fatty acid. While many people think you can only get these from oily fish, this is incorrect. As long as you're eating a balanced diet, you should be able to get the right amount without fretting.

Omega-6 is easy enough to find – it's in most vegetable oils and plant-based butters and margarines, nuts, seeds and green leafy veg. Omega-3 is a little more elusive, but is found in Brussels sprouts, oils, including perilla oil, algal oil and flax oil, walnuts, flax seeds, hemp seeds and chia seeds.

Now, I know the prevalence of seeds in this section may make you recoil. I remember, before I was vegan, feeling sorry for those people who, for some inexplicable reason, wanted to forgo 'real' food and eat like birds or squirrels. Why snack on seeds when you can snack on cheese, I wondered?

But it's important to note that you don't have to be a health freak to get the right amounts of omega-3 in your diet. Because ground flax seeds and chia seeds are available in most supermarkets, it's so easy to add a spoonful to your cereal, yogurt or porridge in the morning. If you're not a breakfast person, just add a spoonful to a shake, whether that's a healthy protein and fruit-packed shake, or an indulgent peanut butter and chocolate shake. It counts, either way. And because less than 30g (1oz) of chia seeds can exceed your recommended daily intake of omega-3 – that's only about two spoonfuls – there's no reason why junk food vegans shouldn't be able to get their essential fatty acids too.

How to Stay Healthy, Fit and Strong –
Some Professional Advice

Once I'd become accustomed to a vegan diet,
I massively overhauled the way I ate. I was tired
of being a junk food vegan; I wanted to set a good
example, to prove you could build muscle and be
strong and fit without consuming animal products.
(I have a vision of someone asking me the ubiquitous
'But what about protein?' question, and answering it
by slowly rolling up my sleeves and flexing, to loud
intakes of breath and rapturous applause.)

But as someone who used to think nothing of
eating six balls of mozzarella on the trot, and
who, even as a vegan, never really cared much
about health, this was new territory. I knew that a
wholefood plant-based diet was the healthiest way to
eat, but I'd never had the impetus to change the way
I ate, to move away from all the processed stuff and
start thinking about what I was putting in my body.
I never questioned whether I was getting the right
nutrients, never wondered what the effect of eating
so much processed food would be.

To help me, I turned to vegan personal trainer
and nutritionist Paul Kerton (aka the Hench
Herbivore). It was Paul who helped me understand
the real benefits of eating this way. And after
following his advice, I can say, hand on heart,
I've never felt better. I have more energy, my skin

is better and I'm building muscle faster than I imagined. Turns out eating healthily and working out really works! Shocker.

For the record, before I 'got healthy', I didn't take any supplements, nor did I fuss about getting the right nutrients. And I still felt fine. Now, I'm not advocating doing this, but in my personal experience, staying 'relatively' healthy as a vegan is easier than you think. You're not going to suddenly keel over if you cut out all animal products. But what I have learned is that if you take extra care, you'll feel bloody fantastic – as in, walking down the street grinning because you feel so good.

So, because I'm not a nutritionist or a personal trainer and Paul is, here's some actual expert advice on starting out as a vegan – as well as what to eat if you're looking to build muscle.

QUESTION: WHAT'S THE BEST WAY FOR A PROSPECTIVE VEGAN TO START OUT?

Paul Kerton: *'If you want to switch from a standard Western diet to a vegan diet (particularly a healthy one that's rich in fibre), it can be beneficial to take a little time over it – perhaps a few weeks. One reason for this is the issue of our gut microbiome. The bacteria that live in our colons is unique to each individual and is predicated on the foods we've eaten. If we've been eating a lower-fibre diet, as many omnivores do, we won't have a high quantity* of the prevotella strains of bacteria that are required to process fibre. So if we suddenly start eating lots more beans, fruits and vegetables, we'll likely experience excess gas, bloating, gut motility disturbances and possibly even pain. What happens then is that the would-be vegan says, 'My body can't handle all this vegan food!', and goes back to their bad habits.

'Their body isn't at fault – they simply didn't give their gut microbiome time to adjust. If they'd decreased some of the unhealthy foods and increased more fibre-rich foods each week, they would have had success.'

QUESTION: WHAT FOODS SHOULD NEW VEGANS INCORPORATE INTO THEIR DIETS IMMEDIATELY?

Paul Kerton: 'Your diet should feature plenty of legumes, wholegrains, fruits (berries are particularly rich in antioxidants), vegetables ('eat the rainbow', but emphasize dark leafy greens for their mineral density and vitamin K), and nuts and seeds (particularly ground flax and chia seeds for their omega-3).

'Use herbs and spices liberally. Not only can they transform otherwise bland dishes into mouthwatering masterpieces, but they're true superfoods – extremely dense nutritionally. My favourite is turmeric, which is the spice with the most data backing up its healthfulness. It fights cancer in three different ways and is highly anti-inflammatory, which is great for exercise recovery. Pair with a pinch of black pepper to amplify its effects.'

QUESTION: WHAT SHOULD NEW VEGANS WATCH OUT FOR, NUTRIENT-WISE – AND SHOULD THEY TAKE SUPPLEMENTS?

Paul Kerton: *'If we're eating a predominantly wholefood plant-based diet with adequate calories and variety, there should be very few nutrients of concern. In terms of basic supplementation, it's wise for most people, but vegans in particular, to eat foods fortified with vitamin B12, or to take a supplement. During times with little or no sunlight exposure, a vitamin D3 supplement becomes necessary. I like to include seaweed daily, to ensure I reach the minimum recommended daily amount (RDA) of iodine. But for people who find seaweed distasteful, an iodine/iodide supplement also works.'*

QUESTION: WHAT SHOULD VEGANS EAT IF THEY'RE LOOKING TO BULK UP OR MAKE SOME #PLANTBASEDGAINS?

Paul Kerton: *'For a strength or physique athlete, the inclusion of a vegan protein powder supplement could be beneficial. Any will do the job and vegan ones are just as effective as the non-vegan ones. Quick and easy protein-packed meals that are high in other key minerals and vitamins are:*

- Tofu scramble with sweet potatoes and greens
- Refried beans with salad on wholegrain rice
- Wholegrain pitta bread or wraps with hummus and salad

- Red lentil pasta with a jar of tomato-based pasta sauce, peas and sweetcorn
- Tofu or tempeh and vegetable stir-fry with quinoa
- Miso soup with wholegrain noodles, vegetables and tofu
- Smoothie with oats, dates, seeds and berries, or tropical fruits with white beans (you can't taste them, I swear!) or a scoop of protein powder.

'Remember that the biggest and strongest animals and – most importantly – the ones who live the longest are, and have always been, herbivorous. We can have it all – an awesome physique AND optimal health! Why on earth would we want to eat any other way?'

Eating and Cooking

What do we eat? What *can* we eat? It's one thing to list a whole bunch of ingredients, but how do you cook them? What do you make? What products do you buy when you go shopping? How do you restock your kitchen?

As with every other aspect of veganism, what you buy, cook and eat is a learning curve. Someone once said to me that I must spend half my life reading labels. I really, really don't – but it's true that in those first few weeks, you'll spend more time than you used to staring at the backs of food packets. But this doesn't last. Soon, you'll know exactly which products and brands are vegan, and once you know, it's second nature. You won't even have to think about it. And because most ingredients you need to look out for are allergens, such as milk traces and eggs, they always appear in bold type in the ingredients list, so it's not like this takes a long time. It's a few extra seconds – a small price to pay for eating more ethically.

While going vegan wasn't hard for me, there were definitely times during the first few weeks when I thought, 'Well, what do I eat?' There were aspects of cooking I had to relearn – how to make a plant-based white sauce, for example, or how to get that intensely savoury (dare I say 'meaty'?) depth of flavour in dishes like lasagne, chilli or shepherd's pie – but this is such a positive. I now cook with ingredients I didn't know existed a few years ago. I enjoy flavours I'd never tasted. When I open my refrigerator I'm excited about the things I can make. The food inside is colourful and fresh and healthy (mostly!). It's a garden, not a graveyard. That's nice.

Make it Easy for Yourself

All you need to succeed is to prepare. Fill up your refrigerator with plant-based products before you start; that way, when you open it, you will have countless different options. Head to your local supermarket and find the veggie/vegan aisle. Find your nearest health food shop and have a browse. This is the fun part! Everyone likes trying new food and you're about to discover just how delicious plant-based food is these days. Most supermarkets stock vegan versions of everything: pizza, sausages, burgers, ice cream. Stock up on products, see what you like. Take a look at Chapter 6 for more ideas.

THE VEGAN COMMUNITY – AKA THE V-GANG – IS HUGE, DIVERSE, WARM AND WELCOMING.

Having a few go-to vegan meals that are delicious and easily rustled up from ingredients you already have is invaluable. What really helped me here was YouTube. Search for 'easy vegan recipes' and see which meals tickle your fancy. I'm a good vegan cook *now*, but I wasn't when I started – and for that I owe YouTube and the many plant-based vloggers who upload their cooking videos.

Learn to 'Veganize'

Even if you're not planning on switching to full vegan just yet, it's still a good idea to introduce as many plant-based products into your diet as possible. Practise recipes, discover which sausages are your favourite, try different plant milks and cheeses and see which ones are for you. This way, you're still learning about vegan food and getting familiar with a plant-based diet – and when you do make the change, you'll already know which products and recipes you like best.

One thing that surprised me when I went vegan is that my favourite meals didn't change. I loved all forms of pasta, tacos, pizza, spicy noodle soups – and I still do. You don't have to alter the things you like to eat – you just have to change a few ingredients. Anything can be veganized. Anything. Steak, foie gras, tuna mayo – you name it, we've veganized it.

At some point, someone will probably ask you why vegans like to replicate or re-create dishes that traditionally contain animal products. The thought process seems to be, 'If you want to eat plants, don't dare try to make them look or taste or feel like meat! You have your food, we have ours. Stick to vegetables!' My answer to this is that vegans don't stop eating meat or cheese or eggs because we don't like the taste. We stop eating them because we oppose the harm they cause. If we can eat something that tastes like the foods we used to enjoy but is infinitely less damaging, why shouldn't we?

Anyway – back to veganizing. During your first few weeks of trying a plant-based diet, don't feel the need to prepare elaborate dishes that require obscure ingredients. It will feel much easier if you stick to some of your favourite dishes and veganize them. That way, it won't feel like your whole world has shifted.

So if you're a spaghetti bolognese fan, cook up some spag bol – just swap the mince for vegan mince or lentils, and grate some plant-based cheese on top. Fajitas? Fill them with veggies, plant-based meat or tofu. Curries? Same applies. Like a fry-up in the morning? Use veggie sausages and bacon, experiment with scrambled tofu, throw in some extra avocado, beans and tomatoes. Love a ploughman's sandwich for lunch? Use vegan mayo and cheese and you probably won't even tell the difference.

You may have noticed there were quite a few processed alternatives in my suggestions above, such as mock meats and vegan cheeses. While a wholefood plant-based diet is the healthiest and most eco-friendly option, there's nothing wrong with eating some vegan alternatives, especially when you start out.

We all learn along the way, and everyone has their own journey. Do what feels best and easiest for you.

Vegan Kitchen Essentials

When you first start looking into vegan cooking, you may find that certain ingredients keep cropping up – and often you'll have never heard of them. Don't be put off by this. The ingredients you use and the dishes you make will expand naturally over time, but to make those first few weeks as easy as possible, there are some items that are definitely worth buying.

As long as you have a few key ingredients in the house, you'll always be able to rustle up some quick yet healthy dinners. Add the following to your next shop:

REFRIGERATOR

Plant milk If you're not a fan of plant milk you probably haven't tried the right one. There's soya, oat, coconut, rice, almond, hemp, cashew, hazelnut and sunflower. Experiment and see what you like. I like oat milk in my coffee, soya milk in my tea and almond or coconut milk for cooking.

Tofu In my experience, people who don't like tofu have just had bad tofu. With so many different styles (firm, silken, puffed) and flavours (smoked, spiced, basil) there's definitely one out there for you. Packed with protein, it also contains all nine essential amino acids, iron, calcium, selenium, magnesium, zinc and Vitamin B1. Boom.

Seitan If you find yourself craving meat, try some seitan; this super-high-protein mock meat can have a disturbingly meaty texture. Cans of seitan, and seitan burgers and sausages are pretty easy to find in big supermarkets, but DIY recipes can also be found online.

Tempeh Think of tempeh as tofu's even healthier big sister. While it's also made from soya beans, tempeh contains whole beans that are fermented, is less processed and contains less fat. It has a more distinct flavour too: an earthy, mushroomy taste. It's not for everyone, so maybe try it cooked in a marinade of your choice the first time.

Miso paste Perfect for adding that umami flavour to sauces, soups and stews. It's also protein rich and a good source of vitamins B, E and K, and folic acid. Because it's fermented, it's good for your gut too.

STORECUPBOARD

Nutritional yeast An essential ingredient for all vegan kitchens. Get ready to make nutritional yeast – or 'nooch' as it's affectionately called – your new best friend. These yellowy yeast flakes add a lovely, cheesy flavour to your food – and because it's a complete protein, contains minerals, such as zinc and selenium, and is packed with B vitamins, it's as healthy as it is delicious. Be sure to get the fortified brands that also contain vitamins B6 and B12. Use it in scrambled tofu, creamy sauces, lasagne, soups and sprinkled on top of pasta – it's an all-rounder.

Nut butters A delicious and easy way to get your protein. Have it on toast or in smoothies and shakes. Nut butters are a great source of fibre, antioxidants, vitamins and healthy fats.

Lentils A plant-based kitchen isn't complete without lentils. High in iron and folates and a great source of protein, they're filling yet low in calories. You can buy dried lentils, tins of lentils in liquid, or shrink-wrapped ready-to-eat lentils.

Beans The beauty of beans is their variety: baked beans on toast; black beans, pinto beans and kidney beans in Mexican-inspired dishes; butter beans, cannellini beans and broad beans in lighter, Mediterranean dishes and so on. Then there's also the mighty chickpea, which gives us another vegan favourite – hummus. A delicious way to get your protein and fibre fix.

Tinned tomatoes Not exactly uncharted territory, but tinned tomatoes are an essential for any plant-based kitchen. When you've got nothing in the house

ALWAYS REMEMBER THAT VEGANISM IS NOT A PURSUIT FOR PERFECTION

except for a few tins, tomatoes can form the base of many healthy, tasty dishes – pasta sauces, spicy chilli, hearty stews, warming casseroles. Plus, they're a great source of antioxidants, vitamins C and K, potassium and folate.

Quinoa Before I went vegan I turned my nose up at quinoa – now I *love* it. It's incredibly versatile: you can add it to salads, stews, soups, porridge and buddha bowls; you can make burgers from it; you can bake it into cakes and brownies to make treats that bit healthier. It's also a superfood, packed with protein and containing all nine essential amino acids. It's high in fibre, magnesium, B and E vitamins, iron, potassium, calcium, phosphorus and antioxidants. The Incas didn't call quinoa the 'mother of all grains' for nothing.

Pasta/Noodles So simple, yet so delicious. Pasta is my favourite food – to me, it's never boring. Part of its appeal is its adaptability, and it's a great way to make sure you're getting other vital nutrients in. From simple tomato and veggie-mince pasta sauces to lentil lasagnes and Asian noodle soups crammed with vegetables and tofu, you can rustle up all kinds of delicious dishes with pasta as your base. Try red lentil pasta, chickpea pasta or spinach pasta to be that bit healthier. Remember, dry pasta is always vegan; fresh pasta usually contains eggs, so keep an eye out.

Chocolate Contrary to popular belief, you don't have to give up chocolate when you go vegan. Most dark chocolate is 'accidentally vegan' anyway (cocoa butter doesn't contain milk) but if you're not a fan of the dark stuff, try the great new plant-based milk chocolate on the market. When I'm trying to be healthy, having a few squares of high-quality dark chocolate helps keep sugar cravings at bay – plus, it's a powerful source of antioxidants.

Nuts When you need a snack, nuts are one of the healthiest choices. High in protein and good fats, nuts have a host of other benefits. Almonds are high in calcium, fibre, vitamin E and magnesium. Cashews are rich in iron and magnesium. Walnuts are packed with omega-3 fats and antioxidants. Hazelnuts are high in magnesium, calcium and vitamins B and E. Peanuts have the highest amount of folates of all the nuts and are rich in vitamin E.

Dates Another healthy snack – especially if you have a sweet tooth. Rich in antioxidants and magnesium, dates also help maintain bone mass, contain a brain booster, and can help reduce blood pressure. They're great on their own, but I like to add chopped dates to porridge, yogurt and smoothies to make them that bit sweeter.

Soy cream/oat cream If, like me, you're a fan of creamy pasta dishes, stock up on some cartons of oat cream or soy cream – they'll keep for months in the cupboard, unopened. Use to make veggie carbonara-type dishes, or pour over berries or cake for dessert – coconut milk is also great for this.

FREEZER

Vegan mince A freezer necessity for those times you want a quick spaghetti bolognese or chilli non carne. Usually made from soya protein or mycoprotein, veggie mince is a complete protein that's low in fat, high in fibre and totally cholesterol free. Just double check to make sure there's no added egg white.

Vegan burgers, sausages and pies So helpful for those times when you get home late and can't be bothered to cook. Most supermarkets sell all kinds of frozen plant-based products, from fishcakes to goujons to chicken-style strips, and almost all are high in protein. When I'm too tired to cook I just chuck a few in the oven and eat them with a big salad. It's super quick, and still pretty healthy.

Frozen peas The humble pea is another plant-based powerhouse. High in protein and fibre, peas are rich in health-boosting antioxidants and contain many key vitamins, minerals and antioxidants too. Perfect for stirring through creamy pasta sauces, making soups, adding to curries, or just serving alongside mashed potato and some vegan sausages.

Ice creams Vegans don't have to make do with sorbet any more. Choose from ice cream made with coconut milk, cashew milk, almond milk or soya milk. Even Ben & Jerry's do plant-based ice cream now, so don't worry about missing out.

Frozen garlic, chilli and ginger Using fresh is always best, but having some chopped garlic, chilli and ginger in the freezer can be an absolute game-changer. No one likes bland food, and if you're low on fresh ingredients, these make all the difference.

VEGAN LIFE

I have no doubts that going vegan, if you do choose to do so, will be one of the best decisions you ever make. But of course, it is a major life change, and it doesn't come without some difficulties. The hard part of being vegan isn't having to look at labels. It isn't having fewer options when you're eating out. It isn't even giving up certain foods you once loved. The hardest part of being vegan is dealing with people who want to bring you down. It's handling the fact that some people are actually angry about the fact that you don't want to eat animals. It's getting a handle on yourself when people feel the need to challenge a decision that's based only on facts, kindness and common sense.

The good news is that as veganism continues to skyrocket, the number of people who actually do these things is dwindling. The bad news is that there are still idiots everywhere – people who'll delight in waving meat under your nose, smacking their lips and saying 'Mmmm bacon!', or sending you photos of their bloody steak.

There can also be changes in the way that you see certain people. Absolutely nothing has changed with my close friends, vegan or otherwise, but there has been a shift regarding the people with whom I want to surround myself. There are some people in my life who say they love animals but refuse point-blank to face the facts about what happens. They won't watch any videos. They won't read an article. On social media they post photos of themselves hugging lambs and say how much they love them; that evening they post a picture of their lamb chops.

Honestly, I do find this difficult. For me, personally, it's one thing if someone confronts certain realities about animal agriculture but doesn't feel ready to make the switch – or maybe doesn't think they ever can. Almost all vegans have been at this stage before. There are also some people who know the facts and simply aren't bothered enough by them to make a change. As much as I oppose this viewpoint, at least it's an informed decision. What does bother me is when people deliberately bury their heads in the sand and refuse to look, and then have the gall to call themselves animal lovers. Because I can't respect that decision, I've found myself naturally drifting from certain people in my life. It's possible that this might happen to you too. Some people will just be on a different vibration from you. And that's okay. It's all part of our personal growth.

On the plus side, as you drift from certain people, you'll bond with others. The vegan community is huge, welcoming, and it's a joy to be part of. When you meet someone else who's vegan there's an instant bond. It's wonderful. There are so many small joys in everyday life. I find myself smiling at the people browsing the vegan section in the supermarket. When I see people who are clearly not vegan looking at new plant-based products and putting them in their trolley, I feel irrationally fond of them. When I see people buying meat but also Quorn, I feel hopeful.

I was recently in the supermarket and saw an elderly couple browsing the plant-based milks. 'Get almond,' the man said. He must have been around eighty – so not your typical vegan. 'I like almond.'

'No, we'll get oat,' his wife replied, 'It's better for the environment.' I had to physically stop myself from flinging my arms around them.

I've made lifelong friends since going vegan. I've had my mind opened. I'm inspired, constantly, by the actions of others. I have more purpose, more drive, more positivity about myself. I love it – and you will too.

Talking to People

But let's be real: if you make the switch to veganism, you will be questioned about it. Some people will be curious, genuinely interested in the reasons why you're making the change – but others will try to find the chink in your armour. Some people just won't understand and will challenge, often angrily, everything you say. If you're someone who shrinks from confrontation, this can be unwelcome and distressing. So how do you deal with it?

———

THE REALITY IS, IT CAN NEVER BE A 'PERSONAL CHOICE' IF THERE'S A VICTIM INVOLVED.

———

First things first: always try to stay calm. Don't judge, and don't get angry (save it up and vent to your vegan friends). Remember that most people are, on the whole, good people – even the ones who love slating veganism. Most people don't actively *want* to hurt animals, but we've also been conditioned not to question the things we do to living beings in the name of food. Confronting the reality of what we're doing to sentient animals – totally unnecessarily –

can be extremely unsettling. It's understandable that some people push back.

Try to understand as best you can. By being calm, compassionate and presenting rational arguments, you're not only destroying the 'angry vegan' trope, but you're also getting the other person thinking. Debate and conversation are powerful tools. And the great thing about debating veganism is that there's no counterargument against it. A meaningful argument against veganism simply does not exist in 2019.

Even if you're someone who hates conflict, as long as you arm yourself with some key facts and remain calm, there's nothing to worry about. In this chapter we're going to look at some of the most commonly asked questions or statements about veganism, and how to reply to them. Chances are, with a bit of practice, debating veganism will become something you really enjoy.

Vegan Counterarguments

#1: WHERE DO YOU GET YOUR PROTEIN FROM?

Let's start with one of the most commonly asked questions – and you should know the answer to this one by now!

The fear of protein deficiency is entirely unfounded. In developed countries, protein deficiency is never an issue. Have you ever in your life heard of someone being protein deficient? Vitamin B12 deficient – sure. Vitamin D deficient – sure. But protein? Never in a million years.

Because almost all foods contain protein, if you're getting enough calories and eating a balanced diet, you'll get enough protein no matter what. Plants, grains and legumes contain all the protein we need. It's always good to namedrop some of the ever-increasing number of plant-based athletes: when people hear that Novak Djokovic, Lewis Hamilton, the Williams sisters and even Arnie all advocate a vegan diet, they tend to accept that protein isn't only found in animal flesh.

#2: OTHER ANIMALS EAT ANIMALS, SO WHY CAN'T WE?

You'll hear this one a lot, and many variations of it. It's one of my favourite arguments against veganism simply because it's so illogical.

This is the only situation where we look at animals in the wild to judge what we should and shouldn't be doing. I've lost count of the times I've heard, 'Lions eat meat, why can't I?' But the actions of wild animals are not a good basis for human morality. Human beings aren't lions, so comparing ourselves to them, or any other carnivorous animal is, frankly, a ludicrous argument. Let's break it down.

Firstly, lions are obligate carnivores, which means they *need* to eat meat to survive. Human beings don't – and as we've seen, eating meat actually causes us a whole host of health problems.

We pay other people to kill animals for us, and we do it for pleasure, because we like the taste of their flesh. Killing for survival and killing for pleasure are two very different things.

Secondly, choosing the one single aspect of lion behaviour you want to emulate while ignoring everything else is an unfair comparison. Lions also habitually kill their own cubs; could a human kill their child, then defend their actions on the basis that lions kill their cubs? Of course not.

Thirdly, as human beings we possess something called moral agency. This means that we have the ability to know right from wrong and can be held accountable for our actions. Lions and other wild animals don't possess moral agency. Lions don't feel guilt when they kill another lion, or when they force themselves sexually on lionesses. Trying to justify our behaviour by comparing ourselves to wild animals with no moral agency is invalid and illogical.

#3: VEGANISM IS UNNATURAL BECAUSE HUMANS HAVE ALWAYS EATEN MEAT.

The idea that veganism is 'unnatural' seems to stem from the fact that (most) humans have eaten meat for thousands of years. This means we're 'supposed' to eat meat, doesn't it?

It's true that humans have eaten meat for thousands of years – but the only reason we began eating meat is because we had to: eating an entirely plant-based diet obviously wasn't possible back in the Iron Age. Nowadays we can easily live without animal products.

Looking to the past to justify our current behaviour is dangerous, because historically humans have done many things we don't condone today. We've always murdered, raped and pillaged, but that doesn't justify doing it today. The whole reason we've progressed as a society is that we looked at our harmful actions and questioned whether they were moral or acceptable. That's how humanity evolved.

We've evolved as a species: we no longer live in caves or make human sacrifices or believe the world is flat. Trying to justify harmful behaviour today by saying 'But we've always done it!' is the equivalent of sticking your finger up at human evolution.

#4: VEGANISM IS UNNATURAL BECAUSE HUMANS HAVE CANINE TEETH.

Ahh, the old teeth argument – the idea that having canines justifies continuing to eat animals. Yes, human beings do have canines, but if you compare human canines to the teeth of any other animal that eats meat, whether omnivore or carnivore, you'll see that ours are significantly smaller, flatter and blunter.

It's also worth mentioning that having big canines doesn't mean you're supposed to eat meat. The biggest canines of any land animal belong to the hippopotamus, and hippos are herbivorous.

Even if we did have long, sharp canines like a lion, it still doesn't mean we 'should' eat animals – because possessing the ability to do something doesn't provide the moral justification to do it.

Men usually have the ability to physically overpower and hurt women – yet we all agree that just because they can, doesn't mean they should.

Just because we possess the ability to chew meat and digest meat, doesn't mean we must kill animals and eat them.

#5: VEGANISM ISN'T ACTUALLY SUSTAINABLE BECAUSE...

While it's well known that meat production has a devastating effect on the environment, recently there's been some bizarre pushback against veganism being sustainable. For example, it's being claimed that soya is harmful to the environment, therefore veganism is bad.

Veganism isn't perfect – what is? – but the facts against meat and dairy are incontrovertible. As we've seen, animal agriculture is the leading cause of ocean

TRYING TO JUSTIFY HARMFUL BEHAVIOUR TODAY BY SAYING 'BUT WE'VE ALWAYS DONE IT!' IS THE EQUIVALENT OF STICKING YOUR FINGER UP AT HUMAN EVOLUTION

dead zones, habitat destruction, species extinction and water pollution (see page 33). Land the size of seven football pitches is razed every minute to make room for livestock; forty per cent of all grain produced globally is used to feed farm animals. Only six per cent of soya is used for human consumption, while more than eighty per cent is used for animal feed.

Some people seem to think that veganism is unsustainable because in a vegan world, there would be too many animals. If everyone went plant based, this belief goes, the world will be overrun with cows, pigs and chickens.

A staggering number of people don't seem to know that we breed these animals into existence for the sole purpose of killing them. The more people switch to plant-based alternatives, the more the demand for animal products will drop. This means fewer animals will be bred into existence. It'll be a slow, gradual progression.

If someone is still trying to challenge the idea that veganism is unsustainable, I usually just say something along the lines of:

'Scientists behind the world's biggest study on the effect of animal agriculture state that avoiding meat and dairy is the single biggest way to reduce your impact on earth. All vegans want to do is to minimize harm – to animals and the environment. If you know of any other way to reduce your impact on the planet that's MORE effective than going vegan, then by all means, let's hear it!'

#6: EATING MEAT IS MY PERSONAL CHOICE. I RESPECT YOUR CHOICE NOT TO EAT MEAT, SO YOU SHOULD RESPECT MINE TOO!

This is something I hear a lot but it's illogical in two ways.

Firstly, asking vegans to respect your decision to eat meat is on par with asking feminists to respect sexists, or asking non-racists to respect racists. It is ludicrous to believe that differences in opinion merit mutual respect when the opposing opinion stands for everything you're against, causes unfathomable pain, and upholds cruelty and exploitation.

Secondly, about that 'personal choice'. It's not a personal choice. A personal choice is something that affects only you – like deciding to dye your hair a certain colour, or choosing to stop drinking alcohol. The minute someone else is harmed by your 'personal choice', it stops being 'personal'.

Let's say I come across a stray dog on the street. Maybe I don't like dogs, and I decide to kill it. Is that my 'personal choice'? What about the choice of the dog not to be harmed or killed? Or is it only human beings who are allowed to have personal choice? People are furious and disgusted when trophy hunters (legally) kill giraffes and lions in Africa – but doing so is the poachers' personal choice.

All manner of sins can be justified by saying, 'Hey, it's my personal choice!' The reality is, it can never be a 'personal choice' if there's a victim involved.

#7: VEGANS JUST GO ON ABOUT BEING VEGAN ALL THE TIME.

We've all heard the old joke, 'How do you know someone's vegan? Don't worry, they'll tell you.' It was funny – the first time. Not so much the 486th time!

Vegans can, and often do, talk about it quite a lot, but the idea that we go running around randomly announcing it to people is silly. Let's take a second to clear this up.

When I went vegan I did tell my family and close friends (it would be really weird if I'd kept it to myself), but all other times I've told people that I'm vegan is because it's relevant – for example, people have offered me a slice of cake, or I'm at a new restaurant and want to know what I can eat. There are lots of reasons why vegans talk about being plant based, but a few of them are:

- Most social situations revolve around food, and mentioning you don't eat animal products is just sensible if you want to be able to eat something.
- Vegans want to normalize being vegan. We don't want people to think we're all dreadlocked hippies clad in hemp. By telling people, we're hoping others see how diverse and inclusive this movement really is – how there's no such thing as a 'typical vegan'.
- Most people are unaware of the cruelty involved in the foods they eat. If telling people you're vegan invites conversation, questions or debate, then vegans welcome that.

- People have a tendency to talk about things that are important to them. They want to share their values, the things they care about.

'I'm fine with people being vegan, just don't shove it in my face.' This is a sentiment I've heard a lot. It makes me think of those times when some people would say they're 'fine' with people being gay as long as they don't 'flaunt it'. Of course, no one was really flaunting it. A same-sex couple walking down the street aren't flaunting anything – they're just living their lives. It's the same with veganism. Vegans are just living their lives – but because their life choices are not those of the majority, they're noticed – and sometimes challenged.

TAKING IT FURTHER

So what now? Well, if you've decided you want to move towards a more vegan way of living, you now have a choice: do you want to be vegan or plant based? Because while the two terms are seen as synonymous, they're not the same thing. Plant based is a diet. Vegan is a way of life.

When Donald Watson coined the term 'veganism' back in 1944, he explained that it meant 'a way of living which seeks to exclude, as far as is possible and practicable, all forms of exploitation of, and cruelty to, animals for food, clothing or any other purpose.' Veganism, in its purest form, is about animals and ethics. It extends far deeper than just what you eat – but this is where most people start.

If you're plant based, you may eat a vegan diet but you won't necessarily actively avoid other forms of animal exploitation. You may not see a problem with wearing fur or leather. You might not have issues with animal testing. If your motivation is simply to be healthier and animals don't really factor into it, then simply eating a plant-based diet might be enough for you. But let's assume, like most people, that you do like animals. That you do want to avoid harming them. Let's assume you want to be vegan – well, we've come this far together! If this is the case, then avoiding harming or exploiting animals by changing your diet is merely the first step. Vegans exclude, as best they possibly can, all forms of animal exploitation from their lives. This extends to what they wear, what they buy, and what they do.

Vegans don't buy or wear fur, leather, suede or anything that comes from an animal. Just as we don't believe animals should be killed for food, we also don't believe they should be killed for fashion. Animals don't care whether they're slaughtered for their fur or their meat, whether they end up in your sandwich or on your feet. They just wish it didn't happen at all.

Vegans don't agree with animal testing, which means we try to buy toiletries or cosmetics that are branded as cruelty free. Because we don't believe animals are here to gratify us, most vegans also avoid aquariums, circuses that use animals, and even zoos. It's true that zoos promote an interest in animals, but the bottom line is that animals are still caged for our benefit.

Now, I know that just making the decision to follow a vegan diet can seem incredibly daunting and scary, without thinking about these additional factors.

Do your very best and remember the reasons why you're doing it, but don't be afraid to go at your

VEGANISM IS ABOUT COMPASSION, SO MAKE IT YOUR MISSION TO TREAT PEOPLE WITH KINDNESS

own pace. Always keep in mind that veganism isn't a pursuit for perfection. If you're struggling just to get to grips with this new way of eating, let yourself adapt to that before taking the next step.

Chances are you probably have leather in your wardrobe, from shoes to belts to bags. Maybe you own fur. Your cushions and pillows might be made from down. Do you have to throw them all out? Well, no. You should do whatever feels right for you. This is your journey. When I made the switch to veganism I knew I no longer wanted to wear anything that came from an animal, but I also didn't have the money to go out and replace all my clothes and accessories at once. So I phased them out. Every time I bought new clothing or a pair of new shoes, I made sure it was made from vegan materials – whether that was vegan leather or recycled plastic or faux suede or cloth.

The fact that you're still wearing a pair of leather boots you've had for years makes no difference to any animal today. What matters is what you're trying to do from now on. What matters is being accountable for the future decisions you make – not being judged for your past choices.

Embracing veganism means embracing every opportunity to reduce the suffering of animals, no matter their species. The biggest tools for advancing veganism, both for yourself and for other people, will always be community, communication and education. So if you're ready to take your veganism further, let's take the next step.

Community

We touched on this earlier (see page 105), but I can't stress it enough – joining groups and following other vegans online is one of the most practical and valuable things you can do. If you're the only vegan you know it can sometimes be a lonely and insular experience, but online you're part of an inclusive, encouraging community. You'll be welcomed with open arms. People will leap at the chance to share their knowledge with you, whether that's which

Everyone can change, but change is usually inspired by positivity and forward momentum, not criticizing people or shaming them.

veggie sausages taste best or which brands do the best cruelty-free toiletries.

Sometimes people feel a bit uneasy about becoming known as 'a vegan'. I know I did. You might feel hesitation over becoming part of a movement that so many still see as extreme – but it's the very act of joining these groups that proves how diverse vegans really are. Becoming part of the vegan community doesn't mean you'll spontaneously sprout dreadlocks. You yourself, and the other vegans you'll meet online, are evidence that vegans cannot be pigeonholed. There's no such thing as a 'typical vegan'. Being vegan doesn't define you. It's not who you are. It's what you believe.

Facebook is one of the best platforms for meeting people and feeling part of something. There are countless vegan groups for different cities and locations, and while you can keep your friendships virtual if you wish, many people meet up regularly, whether to plan activism or just have friendly drinks. You can find out about vegan events and festivals, meet like-minded people, share experiences, get inspired. There are vegan groups for almost every interest, whether you're an athlete or a runner or just a foodie who wants to find out where to eat.

Aside from joining groups, following people on social media is also invaluable. Instagram is especially good for this, particularly for fitness and food inspiration. Cooking for non-vegans and proving how great plant-based food really is is a beautiful form of activism.

Communication

Another reason why social media is so powerful is that it's a huge platform for vegan activism. Activism might be something you shudder at the thought of right now, but it's still helpful to follow activists and learn from them. Talking to non-vegans about veganism can be a hard thing to navigate, but watching conversations between activists and others will help you learn how best to respond. You're arming yourself with the tools necessary to further this cause, without causing unnecessary conflict.

If you only follow one activist, make it Earthling Ed; his calm, compassionate, reasoned way of speaking with people transformed the way I approached this type of conversation. It's so easy to get upset, to become frustrated when you hear the same justifications over and over again – especially when you know better. Becoming exasperated – particularly when you're not given the chance to explain – is easy, but watching a video with Earthling Ed is a lesson in empathetic patience.

Don't tell people why you're right and they're wrong. Instead, ask them questions and let them give you answers. Instead of saying 'There's no such thing as humane meat!', ask 'Do you think there's a humane way to kill an animal who doesn't want to die?' Rather than saying, 'Your taste buds don't justify slaughtering an animal!' ask, 'Do you think enjoying the taste of something is a good enough reason to unnecessarily kill an animal?' When you ask these questions, try to ask them compassionately, without judgement. You don't want to seem confrontational. As soon as the other person becomes defensive, they'll no longer be receptive to what you're saying. Absolutely nobody likes being shamed. You have to allow people to reach their own conclusions themselves. Veganism is about

THE MOST INCREDIBLE THING ABOUT HUMANITY IS OUR ABILITY TO ADAPT AND EVOLVE, TO CHANGE WITH THE TIMES.

compassion, so make it your mission to treat people with kindness.

Remember that no matter how strongly you and another person disagree, no matter how wide the chasm between you seems, there's almost always something powerful that unites you: the belief that animal cruelty is wrong. We all agree with this – but we know that we've been conditioned not to apply this to the animals we eat and exploit. We've all been there. We've all tried to rationalize. We've all looked away. It's easier, and infinitely less painful, than facing the truth.

People mock veganism because they don't understand it, or because they're unaware of the realities of animal agriculture. It's a simple fear of the unknown. Everyone can change, but change is usually inspired by positivity and forward momentum, not criticizing people or shaming them.

Having said that, there is room for all types of activism. People respond to things in different ways, and what works for one might not work for another. Some people do respond better to shock tactics than the positive foodie approach. Often it's seeing shocking footage that inspires people to change, but if you decide to be blunt about what's happening, you can still refuse to be the angry vegan.

Education

Education is power. The more you educate yourself on issues related to veganism, the more influence you'll have when it comes to discussing them. You might be an animal lover who's deeply affected by what happens on farms, but not everyone feels the same. For many people, the environment is a far bigger motivating factor in changing the way they eat; for others, their health comes first. Making sure you're educated about these different factors and the role veganism plays within them means you're always able to discuss what's important to others.

This book is just the tip of the iceberg. Take time to educate yourself about other aspects of veganism, such as not using animals for clothing or scientific research. Today there's a wealth of information at our fingertips, from free documentary films you can watch online to downloadable nutrition guides. In my experience, film is generally the easiest and most effective way to reach people.

Check out the following films to learn more – and to know what to send to people who are open to learning.

Earthlings Made in 2005 and narrated by actor Joaquin Phoenix, *Earthlings* is an American documentary that covers all the different ways in which humans exploit animals, from food and clothing to entertainment and scientific research.

WE DON'T LIVE IN A VEGAN WORLD YET – BUT MAKE NO MISTAKE, IT'S COMING

If you want to go vegan but need that final push, *Earthlings* will probably do it. Known as the original 'vegan-maker' film, it's a powerful and harrowing watch. While it's hard to get through, it will change the way you see the world forever.

The Game Changers One for the health and fitness enthusiasts among us, *The Game Changers* is a 2019 film produced by James Cameron, Arnold Schwarzenegger and Jackie Chan, executively produced by Lewis Hamilton and Novak Djokovic. Following elite athletes and with insight from visionary scientists, this documentary explores the meteoric rise of plant-based eating in sports and exposes outdated meat myths. An enormously inspirational film that will reveal the true strength of plant-based performance.

Dominion This is a 2018 Australian documentary that explores the different ways in which animals are used by humans; because it's a much newer film than *Earthlings*, it's more relevant to modern audiences. Focusing on the legal, industry-standard procedures of animal agriculture, *Dominion* uses hidden camera footage as well as drones to reveal the terrifying truths about an industry built on lies and secrecy. You'll be left questioning the morality of humanity's dominion over all other beings.

Cowspiracy This award-winning documentary made in 2014 follows filmmaker Kip Andersen as he uncovers the devastating impact factory farming has on the environment. *Cowspiracy* is a shocking yet humorous film that explores the effect animal agriculture is having on our planet – and why the world's leading environmental organizations won't talk about it. Inspirational and moving, the film reveals the role big business has played in destroying our planet, while offering a solution to global sustainability.

Land of Hope and Glory If *Dominion* is Australia's *Earthlings*, then *Land of Hope and Glory* is the UK's version. Made in 2017 by the founders of the animal rights organization Surge, this film will dismantle any idealistic notions Brits might have about the system being any better over here. Featuring a hundred British facilities and including up-to-date investigations and never-before-seen undercover footage, *Land of Hope and Glory* reveals the brutal truth behind farming in the UK.

What the Health Branded as the film that health organizations don't want you to see, *What the Health* is the 2017 follow-up film from the creators of *Cowspiracy*. This investigative documentary reveals the fraud and corruption in government and big businesses that's keeping people sick, as well as costing trillions in healthcare dollars. If you were interested in the deception of the meat, dairy and egg industries that we explored in the health section (see page 80), this film is a must-see.

PLANT BASED IS A DIET. VEGAN IS A WAY OF LIFE.

Final Thoughts

So now we've come to the end of our journey. Where you head next is up to you. It might take some time to arrive at your final destination, but beginning to walk the path is the first step. If you do decide to embrace veganism – and I hope you do – it will be a joy, a revelation. If going vegan overnight seems overwhelming, why not take it week by week? In Chapter 6 you'll find simple ideas for transitioning to a plant-based lifestyle – how to prepare, what to expect, and what to do when motivation wanes. It features some simple swaps and sample meal plans – if any of the dishes take your fancy, just Google for the full recipe and ingredients list.

Once you face up to the truth there's no unseeing it. Opening your eyes is one of the most liberating and legitimizing things you can do – but at times it hurts. Sometimes it can seem like progress is happening too slowly. Our planet is running out of time. But never lose sight of the fact that change doesn't happen overnight. As animal activist Gary Yourofsky said: 'It took 400 years to convince white people in America not to own black people. So you can understand why this is taking so long.'

The most incredible thing about humanity is our ability to adapt and evolve, to change with the times, to look at certain behaviours we've always engaged in and be able to recognize that they're harmful, that they're unjust – and stop doing them. It wasn't long ago that we gave women the right to vote, that we started treating all people as human beings, that we allowed LGBTQ+ people to be themselves. But with all these things, change didn't happen overnight.

When compassionate progress is suggested, the first reaction is always to mock and scorn. People don't understand these new, empathic principles, and because they don't, they do the easy thing: they laugh at them instead.

The second stage is rejection and fierce resistance. Changing the status quo is scary. People want things to remain the way they were, and they'll fight until the bitter end to keep the power balance as it is.

The third stage is acceptance.

In the past, it's taken centuries, or even millennia, for change to be truly implemented, but today we have something on our side. With social media and streaming and drone footage, you can't hide the truth any longer. You can try to twist it, to spin it, but it you can't conceal it entirely. And this explains why veganism is the fastest-growing lifestyle movement the world has ever seen. It will not stop.

Change is happening now. Veganism is happening now. If someone had told me two years ago that McDonald's, Burger King and KFC would not only have vegan burgers on their menus, but also be selling out of them, that you could get a vegan menu in almost every chain restaurant, that all the major fashion houses are banning fur, I wouldn't have believed them. But this is our new reality.

We don't live in a vegan world yet – but make no mistake, it's coming. For the sake of our planet, for the sake of the animals, for the sake of our own health, it has to come. And if you ever feel like you're not having an impact, that no matter what you do nothing will ever change, remember that it only takes one to change a few. It takes a few to change many. It takes many to change the world.

But it all starts with one.

FOUR WEEKS TO VEGAN

WEEK 1

1. Sign up to Veganuary

Whatever month you're trying veganism, the best advice is to sign up to Veganuary, a non-profit organization that runs throughout the year. Once you're signed up, you're assigned a mentor and are sent tools and resources to make everything easier – from quick and delicious recipes to facts that'll keep motivation high.

2. Get Your Shopping in

It's vital to have a kitchen filled with delicious food *before* you try going vegan. Check out the list of vegan kitchen essentials in Chapter 3 and stock up on everything you think you'll eat. If you enjoy cooking, buy ingredients that form a key part of wholefood, plant-based cooking, such as chia seeds and nutritional yeast. If not, stock up on easy vegan food you can knock up quickly.

3. Make a Meal Plan

Once you're signed up to Veganuary, you'll be sent free meal plans, but that doesn't mean you can't create your own or see what else is out there. There are gluten-free meal plans, family-friendly meal plans and meal plans for people who only have ten minutes to cook. Have a look online and see which one suits you.

4. *Stock up on Healthy Snacks*

Stock up on snacks – for when you're at home as well as out and about. Vegan food options on the road are still hit-or-miss, so having some healthy snacks such as nuts, dried fruit or energy bars or balls can make all the difference. There are lots of 'accidentally' vegan snacks if you're craving a treat – from Oreos to doughnuts to crisps – so do some research!

SIMPLE SWAP

REPLACE MEAT

The first – and easiest – food swap is switching meat for plant-based sources of protein. Try vegan sausages and burgers, experiment with mock meats and mince, discover the versatility of tofu. And of course, embrace healthy wholefood protein sources – lentils, peas, chickpeas, beans and so on. (Don't forget: no meat also means no fish! It's still animal flesh.)

SAMPLE MEAL PLAN

Breakfast: Wholegrain toast with peanut butter and sliced banana

Lunch: Wrap with hummus, roasted vegetables, spinach and tomato

Dinner: Chilli with beans and/or vegan mince, brown rice, avocado and vegan soured cream

---

WEEK 2

1. Be Generous With Your Portions

Because plant-based foods are generally lower in calories, it's important to ensure you're eating enough. You may find you need bigger portion sizes to feel full – that's great, it means more food! If people say they're always hungry while eating vegan, the reason is simple: they're not eating enough.

2. Invest in a Nutrition Wall Chart

My favourite wall chart is the illustrated Liz Cook nutrition chart, which highlights all the plant-based sources of vitamins and minerals.

3. Take a Supplement

If you're eating a well-planned vegan diet, there's no need to worry about staying healthy. Although many vegan products are already fortified with vitamin B12, set your mind at ease by taking a supplement.

4. Plan Your Lunch

Depending on your job and where you live, lunch can be a tricky meal to navigate. In a city it's easy to grab a vegan lunch; otherwise you may need to plan ahead. Pack a lunch the day before – Google 'quick vegan lunches' for ideas. Or do the easy thing, and make extra dinner the night before.

5. *Figure out Your Go-to Meals*

As you try more plant-based foods, start to figure out what your go-to meals are. What dishes can you knock up quickly when you're tired? What dinners are easy to make when your fridge is empty but your cupboard is full? Remember that it takes experience to become a vegan culinary whizz, so use this early stage to experiment, and have fun adapting meals.

SIMPLE SWAP

REPLACE DAIRY MILK, YOGURT AND ICE CREAM

With the variety of plant milks available, cows' milk is super easy to replace. Try out different plant/nut milks and see which you like best. The same goes for butter, yogurt and ice cream – experiment with brands and flavours.

SAMPLE MEAL PLAN

Breakfast: Overnight oats with berries, banana, maple syrup and milled flax/chia seeds
Lunch: Falafel and hummus with a big salad and pitta bread
Dinner: Stir-fried vegetables and garlic-ginger tofu with rice noodles

---

WEEK 3

1. Give Your Body Time to Adjust

At this stage your body is in detox mode and needs time to adapt. You'll probably notice some changes: some people experience a slight drop in energy, others feel invigorated and strong. The important thing is not to freak out – any negative symptoms will soon pass as your body adjusts. Also, drink lots of water: this makes everything easier.

2. Watch Motivational Videos

There will inevitably be moments when motivation wanes. That's fine – but use those situations to remind yourself *why* you're trying veganism. Watch inspiring films such as *The Game Changers* (see page 163). Check out vegan cooking tutorials on YouTube. Remind yourself of the horrors of animal agriculture. Watch conversations between animal activists and others. The more you know about veganism, the easier it is.

3. Identify Your Local Restaurant Options

Eating out as a vegan is nowhere near as restrictive as you might think. Most restaurants have vegan menus, these days, so have fun trying new vegan dishes. Check out Happy Cow, a free online service that lists all the vegan restaurants near you, and explore which ethnic foods are your favourites (Indian food is usually good for vegans, as is Southeast Asian).

4. Find a Community

Change is easier when you have a buddy. If you don't have any family or friends going vegan with you, explore the virtual vegan community. Join online groups and chat to people. Invite non-vegan friends over and try out your plant-based cooking on them; even if they're not on the same vegan journey as you, that doesn't mean they can't be part of it.

SIMPLE SWAP

REPLACE DAIRY CHEESE

Vegan cheese gets a bad rep, but there are new brands emerging all the time, so there'll be one you love. Try plant-based cream cheeses, Cheddar-style blocks and artisan nut cheeses, and learn to use nutritional yeast in cooking to get that delicious cheesy taste.

SAMPLE MEAL PLAN

Breakfast: Avocado and chickpea on toast with lime and coriander

Lunch: Jacket potato with a mixture of mashed chickpeas, vegan mayo, red onion and nutritional yeast

Dinner: Spicy coconut curry with tofu and veggies, served with quinoa

WEEK 4

1. Ask for Help Online

If you have no clue which vegan cheese to try, or which plant-based yogurts are the creamiest, ask for tips and suggestions – Twitter and Facebook communities are especially useful for this. If you know other vegans, ask for their advice – we love to help out!

2. Try New Ingredients

One of the best things about being plant based is discovering ingredients you'd never heard of and creating delicious meals with them. As you find your feet, become more adventurous. Start stocking up your spice rack, discover which flavours you love, try foods you turned your nose up at before, and become more inventive and daring with your cooking.

3. Own Your Decision

Some people going vegan feel apprehensive about talking about it, but it's important to own your decision. You don't need to be combative, but be confident. If you explain your choice to go vegan with calm rationality and conviction (but no judgement!), you'll earn most people's respect.

4. Be Kind to Yourself

Never forget that veganism isn't a pursuit for perfection. At some point, you'll mess up. Don't sweat it. It's not about being perfect; it's about trying to be better. Always remember that the definition of veganism is a way of life that seeks to avoid animal cruelty 'as far as is possible and practical'. In these early days it won't always seem practical. Other times it might not seem possible. You're taking your first steps on a journey, so be kind to yourself.

SIMPLE SWAP

OMIT ALL ANIMAL PRODUCTS

Okay, this one isn't as easy as the other simple swaps, but now's the time to move to a fully plant-based diet. If eggs are your weakness, try out protein-packed vegan breakfasts where you won't miss them; for baking, replace eggs with chia and flax seeds — they work just as well.

SAMPLE MEAL PLAN

Breakfast: Breakfast burrito with scrambled tofu, black beans, tomatoes, onions and avocado

Lunch: Moroccan chickpea soup with spinach, served with flatbread

Dinner: Pasta with roasted cauliflower in a sauce of cashews, plant milk and nutritional yeast

---

Sources

Chapter 1 My Vegan Journey
1. 'New Sexing Technology to Stop the Culling of Day-old Male Chicks', *Farmers Guardian*, 2 September 2019
2. Humane Slaughter Association, 'Gas Killing of Chicks in Hatcheries', http://www.hsa.org.uk/downloads/technical-notes/TN14-gas-killing-of-chicks-in-hatcheries.pdf (accessed October 2019)

Chapter 2 The Facts
1. Ipsos MORI, 'Vegan Society Poll', 17 May 2016
2. Global Data, 'Top Trends in Prepared Foods 2017', June 2017 (Report ID: 4959853)

THE ENVIRONMENT (PAGES 32–47)
1. Climate Central, 'The 10 Hottest Global Years on Record', 6 February 2019
2. 'The State of Greenhouse Gases in the Atmosphere Based on Global Observations Through 2017', *WMO Greenhouse Gas Bulletin* no. 14, 22 November 2018
3. Jambeck, J R et al, 'Plastic Waste Inputs from Land into the Ocean', *Science Magazine* vol. 347, issue 6223: 768–771, 13 February 2015
4. *Scientific American*, 'Measuring the Daily Destruction of the World's Rainforests', http://www.scientificamerican.com/article/earth-talks-daily-destruction/ (accessed October 2019)
5. Poore, J and Nemecek, T, 'Reducing Food's Environmental Impacts Through Producers and Consumers', *Science Magazine* vol. 360, issue 6392: 987–992, 1 June 2018
6. Thornton, P, Herrero, M and Ericksen, P, 'Livestock and Climate Change', International Livestock Research Institute, issue brief 3, November 2011
7. Poore, J and Nemecek, T, 'Reducing Food's Environmental Impacts Through Producers and Consumers'
8. Hogan, C M, 'Overgrazing', *The Encyclopedia of Earth*, October 2019
9. Eshel, G et al, 'Land, Irrigation Water, Greenhouse Gas, and Reactive Nitrogen Burdens of Meat, Eggs, and Dairy Production in the United States', *Proceedings of the National Academy of Sciences*, 111 (33): 11996–12001, 19 August 2014
10. Poore, J and Nemecek, T, 'Reducing Food's Environmental Impacts Through Producers and Consumers'
11. *Science Daily*, 'Smithsonian Researchers Show Amazonian Deforestation Accelerating', 15 January 2002
12. Worm, B et al, 'Impacts of Biodiversity Loss on Ocean Ecosystem Services', *Science Magazine* vol. 314, 3 November 2006
13. Mood, A and Brooke, P, 'Estimating the Number of Fish Caught in Global Fishing Each Year', Fish Count, July 2010
14. Díaz, S, Settele, J and Brondízio, E, 'Report on Biodiversity and Ecosystem Services', *IPBES Global Assessment*, 6 May 2019
15. Lebreton, L et al, 'Evidence that the Great Pacific Garbage Patch is Rapidly Accumulating Plastic', *Nature Scientific Reports* vol. 8, article number: 4666, 2018
16. Breitburg, D et al, 'Declining Oxygen in the Global Ocean and Coastal Waters', *Science Magazine* vol. 359, issue 6371, 5 January 2018
17. Von Reusner, L, 'Meat Pollution in America: The Industry Behind the Quiet Destruction of the American Heartland', *Mighty Earth*, 2018
18. Keledjian, A, 'Bycatch Report', *Oceana*, March 2014
19. Ibid.
20. Worm, B et al, 'Global Catches, Exploitation Rates, and Rebuilding Options for Sharks', *Marine Policy* vol. 40: 194–204, July 2013

21. World Animal Protection, 'Sea Change: Our Fight Against Ghost Gear', http://www.worldanimalprotection.org.uk/seachange (accessed October 2019)

22. Parker, L, 'The Great Pacific Garbage Patch Isn't What You Think It Is', *National Geographic*, 22 March 2018

23. *Los Angeles Times*, 'To make a burger, first you need 660 gallons of water,' 27 January 2014, http://www.latimes.com/food/dailydish/la-dd-gallons-of-water-to-make-a-burger-20140124-story.html (accessed October 2019)

24. Environmental Working Group, 'Water: Environmental Impact', http://www.ewg.org/meateatersguide/interactive-graphic/water/ (accessed October 2019)

25. Ibid.

26. Richey, AS et al, 'Quantifying Renewable Groundwater Stress with GRACE', *Water Resources Research* vol. 51, issue 7: 5217–5238, July 2015

27. *Six Arguments for a Greener Diet: How a More Plant-based Diet Could Save Your Health and the Environment*, Chapter 4: 'More and Cleaner Water', page 89, Washington, DC: Center for Science in the Public Interest, http://cspinet.org/sites/default/files/attachment/six_arguments_high.pdf

28. Gerbens-Leenes, P W et al, 'The Water Footprint of Poultry, Pork and Beef: A Comparative Study in Different Countries and Production Systems', *Water Resources and Industry* vol. 1–2: 25–36, March–June 2013

29. Food Print, 'How Industrial Agriculture Affects Our Water', http://foodprint.org/issues/how-industrial-agriculture-affects-our-water/ (accessed October 2019)

30. Ibid.

31. A Well-fed World, 'Factory Farms', http://awellfedworld.org/factory-farms/ (accessed October 2019)

32. Williams, M et al, 'The Anthropocene Biosphere', *The Anthropocene Review* (Sage Journals) vol. 2, issue 3, 18 June 2015

33. International Union for Conservation of Nature's Red List of Threatened Species, http://www.iucnredlist.org/ (accessed October 2019)

34. Institute for Agriculture & Trade Policy, 'Emissions Impossible: How Big Meat and Dairy Are Heating Up the Planet', 18 July 2018

35. Grooten, M and Almond, R E A, 'Living Planet Report 2018: Aiming Higher', WWF, 2018

36. Food and Agriculture Organization of the United Nations, 'Livestock's Long Shadow: Environmental Issues and Options', http://www.fao.org/3/a0701e/a0701e00.htm (accessed October 2019)

37. Poore, J and Nemecek, T, 'Reducing Food's Environmental Impacts Through Producers and Consumers'

38. Food and Agriculture Organization of the United Nations, 'Livestock's Long Shadow'

39. Institute for Agriculture & Trade Policy, 'Emissions Impossible'

40. Rainforest Foundation, 'Deforestation in Your Kitchen', http://rainforestfoundation.org/agriculture/ (accessed October 2019)

41. *Scientific American*, 'Measuring the Daily Destruction of the World's Rainforests'

42. Nunez, C, 'Deforestation Explained', *National Geographic*, 7 February 2019

43. Rainforest Foundation, 'Deforestation in Your Kitchen'

44. Union of Concerned Scientists, 'Soybeans', http://www.ucsusa.org/resources/soybeans (accessed October 2019)

45. Pearce, F, 'UK Animal Feed Helping to Destroy Asian Rainforest, Study Shows', *Guardian*, May 2011

THE ANIMALS (PAGES 47–76)

1. Red Tractor Assurance, 'On-farm Humane Killing of Cattle and Sheep', http://assurance.redtractor.org.uk/contentfiles/Farmers-5418.pdf (accessed October 2019)

2. Animal Legal Defence Fund, 'Farmed Animals and the Law', http://aldf.org/focus_area/farmed-animals/ (accessed October 2019)

3. PETA, 'Pigs: Intelligent Animals Suffering on Farms and in Slaughterhouses', http://www.peta.org/issues/animals-used-for-food/animals-used-food-factsheets/pigs-intelligent-animals-suffering-factory-farms-slaughterhouses/ (accessed October 2019)

4. Kendrick, KM et al, 'Sheep Don't Forget a Face', Nature vol. 414: 165–166, November 2001

5. PETA, 'Chickens Used for Food', http://www.peta.org/issues/animals-used-for-food/factory-farming/chickens/ (accessed October 2019)

6. http://www.thetimes.co.uk/article/donald-watson-3w5klz9t0c0

HEALTH (PAGES 76–97)

1. 'Position of the Academy of Nutrition and Dietetics: Vegetarian Diets', Journal of the Academy of Nutrition and Dietetics vol. 116, no. 12, December 2016

2. Kim, H et al, 'Plant-Based Diets Are Associated With a Lower Risk of Incident Cardiovascular Disease, Cardiovascular Disease Mortality, and All-Cause Mortality in a General Population of Middle-aged Adults', Journal of the American Heart Association vol. 8, issue 16, 20 August 2019

3. The Physicians' Committee for Responsible Medicine, 'Health Concerns About Dairy: Avoid the Dangers of Dairy With a Plant-Based Diet', http://www.pcrm.org/good-nutrition/nutrition-information/health-concerns-about-dairy (accessed October 2019)

4. Feskanich, D et al, 'Milk Consumption During Teenage Years and Risk of Hip Fractures in Older Adults', JAMA Pediatr. 168(1): 54–60, January 2014

5. Ludwig, D S and Willett, W C, 'Three Daily Servings of Reduced-Fat Milk: An Evidence-Based Recommendation', JAMA Pediatr. 167(9): 788–9, September 2013

6. Mole, B, 'Milk Alternatives Stunt Kids' Height, Says Doctor with Dairy Industry Ties', Ars Technica, 6 October 2017

7. Paediatric Medicine Research Newsletter, Winter Issue, November 2010–February 2011

8. Carsley, S et al, 'Cohort Profile: The Applied Research Group for Kids', International Journal of Epidemiology, 44(3): 776–788, June 2015

9. Brett, N R et al, 'Dietary Vitamin D Dose-response in Healthy Children 2 to 8 Years of Age: A 12-wk Randomized Controlled Trial Using Fortified Foods', The American Journal of Clinical Nutrition vol. 103, issue 1: 144–152, January 2016

10. Mole, B, 'Milk Alternatives Stunt Kids' Height, Says Doctor with Dairy Industry Ties', Ars Technica, 6 October 2017

11. Cal-in Plus, National Osteoporosis Society, http://www.calinplus.co.uk/national-osteoporosis-society (accessed October 2019)

12. Campbell, D, 'Eating Cheese Does Not Raise Risk of Heart Attack or Stroke, Study Finds', Guardian, 8 May 2017

13. Guo, J et al, 'Milk and Dairy Consumption and Risk of Cardiovascular Diseases and All-cause Mortality: Dose-response Meta-analysis of Prospective Cohort Studies', University of Reading, 27 March 2017

14. The Physicians' Committee for Responsible Medicine, 'Doctors Group Tells Dietary Guidelines Advisory Committee to Ditch Dairy', http://www.pcrm.org/news/news-releases/doctors-group-tells-dietary-guidelines-advisory-committee-ditch-dairy (accessed October 2019)

15. Greger, M, 'Peeks Behind the Egg Industry Curtain', Nutrition Facts, http://nutritionfacts.org/2015/03/26/peeks-behind-the-egg-industry-curtain/ (accessed October 2019)

16. Lia, Y et al, 'Egg Consumption and Risk of Cardiovascular Diseases and Diabetes: A Meta-analysis', *Atherosclerosis Journal* vol. 229, issue 2: 524–530, August 2013

17. United States Department of Agriculture, 'Meat and Poultry Labeling Terms', http://www.fsis.usda.gov/wps/portal/fsis/topics/food-safety-education/get-answers/food-safety-fact-sheets/food-labeling/meat-and-poultry-labeling-terms/meat-and-poultry-labeling-terms (accessed October 2019)

18. Whoriskey, P, 'USDA: We Will Not Steer People Away from Meat to Protect the Environment', *Washington Post*, 7 October 2015

19. Ibid.

20. The Physicians' Committee for Responsible Medicine, 'Processed Meat: There Is No Safe Amount of Processed Meat', http://www.pcrm.org/good-nutrition/nutrition-information/processed-meat (accessed October 2019)

21. http://jamanetwork.com/journals/jamainternalmedicine/fullarticle/414881

22. Lew Q J et al, 'Red Meat Intake and Risk of ESRD', *American Society of Nephrology*, 28(1): 304–312, January 2017

23. Bergeron, N et al, 'Effects of Red Meat, White Meat, and Non-Meat Protein Sources on Atherogenic Lipoprotein Measures in the Context of Low Compared with High Saturated Fat Intake', *American Journal of Clinical Nutrition* vol. 110, issue 3: 783, September 2019

24. Stoiber, T and Naidenko, O, 'Smarter Seafood Choices Can Lower Mercury Exposure for Parents and Their Future Children', *Environmental Working Group*, 10 September 2018

25. Guilford, G, The Future is Here: 'People are Now Eating More Farmed Fish than Wild-caught Fish', *QUARTZ*, 14 July 2016

26. Centers for Disease Control and Prevention, 'Heart Disease Facts', http://www.cdc.gov/heartdisease/facts.htm (accessed October 2019)

27. British Heart Foundation, 'Risk Factors', http://www.bhf.org.uk/informationsupport/risk-factors (accessed October 2019)

28. The Physicians' Committee for Responsible Medicine, 'Lowering Cholesterol with a Plant-based Diet', http://www.pcrm.org/good-nutrition/nutrition-information/lowering-cholesterol-with-a-plant-based-diet (accessed October 2019)

29. Yokoyama, Y et al, 'Association Between Plant-Based Diets and Plasma Lipids: A Systematic Review and Meta-analysis', *Nutrition Reviews* vol. 75, issue 9: 683–98, September 2017

30. Hales, C M et al, 'Prevalence of Obesity Among Adults and Youth: United States, 2015–2016', *National Center for Health Statistics Data Brief* no. 288, October 2017

31. Wikipedia, 'Obesity in the United Kingdom', http://en.wikipedia.org/wiki/Obesity_in_the_United_Kingdom (accessed October 2019)

32. Wikipedia, 'Obesity in Australia', http://en.wikipedia.org/wiki/Obesity_in_Australia (accessed October 2019)

33. Tonstad, S et al, 'Type of Vegetarian Diet, Body Weight, and Prevalence of Type 2 Diabetes', *Diabetes Care*, 32(5): 791–796, May 2009

34. Alexander, S et al, 'A Plant-based Diet and Hypertension', *Journal of Geriatric Cardiology*, 14(5): 327–330, May 2017

35. Toumpanakis, A et al, 'Effectiveness of Plant-Based Diets in Promoting Well-being in the Management of Type 2 Diabetes: A Systematic Review', *BMJ Open Diabetes Research and Care*, 30 October 2018

Chapter 3 Starting Out

1. Capps, A, 'B12: A Magic Pill, or Veganism's Achilles Heel?', *Free From Harm*, 11 April 2014

Index

Acknowledgements

———

Firstly, a huge, heartfelt thank you to everyone, vegan or otherwise, who reads this book, for your open minds. Thank you for wanting to make a difference to our planet and to the lives of animals.

Thank you to everyone at Octopus for giving me this wonderful opportunity – in particular, Stephanie, for believing in this book. Thank you to all at Kruger Cowne – especially Oscar (definitely a future vegan) and Adrian, for having faith in me and believing I could be more than 'a vegan freelancer'. Also thanks to Oscar for putting up with all my Bitmojis.

Thank you to all my friends who've helped out with this book along the way – either with direct advice or for supporting me when I needed it: Tom, Lucy, Laura and Mathew (and Elio), Suki, Dave and Willy, Real, Maria, and *Guardian* bully James D. Special thanks to Plant-Powered Soph, for all her knowledge, empathy and voice notes along the way. She is a far braver vegan than I could ever hope to be. Thank you to Paul Kerton for his advice and inspiration, and thanks to all the other vegan activists out there making a difference – in particular, Earthling Ed and Gary Yourofsky, for helping me see the truth.

Thank you to Tom, for joining me on this vegan journey and being the kindest, most patient and most compassionate plant-based partner. Tom, I told you going vegan would be the best decision you ever made!

About the author

Selene Nelson is a vegan journalist, freelance writer, author and activist, who has written and spoken extensively about food and travel, crime and punishment, and both human and animal rights.